AF574852

HOW TO RUN A TEAROOM

HOW TO RUN A TEAROOM

WINIFRED GRAHAM

PIATKUS

First published in Great Britain in 1981 by
Judy Piatkus (Publishers) Limited of Loughton, Essex

Graham, Winifred.
How to run a tearoom.
1. Restaurant management.
2. Restaurants, lunch rooms, etc.
I. Title
658'.91'64795 TX945

ISBN 0-86188-082-X

Typesetting by V & M Graphics Ltd, Aylesbury, Bucks
Printed by R. J. Acford, Chichester

Contents

INTRODUCTION

If you enjoy cooking and meeting people, have a sense of humour and are not afraid of hard work, then the running of a tearoom may be just the career for you.

More and more people are looking for good home cooking when they eat out. As they tire of brash eating places, which charge exorbitant prices for inferior meals, so they search out small tearooms that serve home-made fare.

Do not think that owning and running a tearoom is merely a hobby, or a job suitable for a school-leaver or for an elderly person wanting an interest outside the home. A successful tearoom requires a proprietor with not only a sound knowledge of human nature, but also good health and a keen interest in and understanding of cooking and the service of food. Running your own tearoom can be an interesting and rewarding way of life; new friends are quickly made and life is far from dull. You have the advantage of being your own boss and knowing that you have an opportunity to express your own personality in your work.

In order to run a tearoom successfully you must be able and willing to carry out any job yourself, from cooking and waiting at the tables, to washing-up and cleaning the floors - so do not think that you can always employ others to do these tasks for you. Your own personality is the trademark of the business so it is poor management to pay someone else to carry out work that you can do yourself.

A good basic training is most important for both owner and staff alike; a cake-making course is a must. Your cakes may be delicious and you may make feather-light pastry and scones, but remember that there are tricks to every trade. Although it may be easy to mix a batch of scones from 1 lb (500 g) flour, it is not so simple when you are dealing with larger quantities and are working to a deadline. You must learn to bake cakes and scones that are always of a consistent size and quality. There must be no guesswork, and all ingredients must be accurately weighed and measured. Cake-making courses are available at many local Technical Colleges and Colleges of Further Education. Some of these colleges run more comprehensive courses in cookery which include cake-making. There may also be part-time courses, ranging from one half-day or evening per week to six days for two or three weeks. Information about the content and timing of the courses and of their cost may be obtained upon application to the college concerned.

In addition to these courses there are, in many colleges, non-vocational classes which cover such subjects as Introduction to Cookery; Adventurous Cooking; Cordon Bleu Cooking; Cake Making and Confectionery and Creative Cooking. Any one of these would be helpful and a useful way of picking up tips for commercial application.

For the really ambitious, basic catering courses, culminating in City and Guilds examinations, must be considered. These courses are run in Technical Colleges and Colleges of Further Education. They are designed for cooks in hotels, restaurants and other catering establishments and are available to those of school-leaving age and over. The subjects covered are varied and are essential for those wishing to make a career within the catering industry, but less training would be sufficient for someone interested in running a tearoom. There seems little point in learning to cater for five hundred people at a banquet when you only wish to serve light snacks in a tearoom seating a few! Course details can be obtained direct from the City and Guilds of London Institute. Further information and advice is also available from the Hotel and Catering Industries Training Board, and from local careers offices, job centres, libraries and colleges.

I would, however, advise anyone wishing to undertake the running of a tearoom to spend perhaps a year training in a similar establishment. Make sure, however, that it is clearly understood from the start that you are there for training purposes and that you are not going to be a 'general dogsbody'.

Another matter to consider when contemplating starting a business is that of partnerships. Only the most independent of people will want to start up in business alone. The most common partnerships are husband and wife teams, and these usually run a business very successfully, provided that one does not have to 'carry' the other. Friends of long standing can work well in partnership, too. A partnership of people with conflicting personalities and opinions is unfortunate and creates an unhappy atmosphere, which customers will quickly notice, often causing them to take their custom elsewhere. Both partners must be willing and able to share the work load as well as the responsibility, so that one can easily take complete control if the other should be ill or away on holiday. This is important, since it ensures that the tearoom can remain open all the year round. It is sometimes useful if one partner is slightly better than the other at cooking, whilst the other partner is better at, and enjoys, the book-keeping side of the business - but there must be a perfect understanding right from the start as to the division of duties.

WHAT TO LOOK FOR WHEN BUYING A TEAROOM

The location of a tearoom is of great importance. Decide where you want to be and in which part of the country, for there is little point in looking for premises in a town when you would rather work in country surroundings, or vice versa. Do not expect to start with large premises; always gain experience running a small tearoom first.

There are, of course, advantages and disadvantages to both town and country positions. In towns, although the purchase price and running costs will tend to be higher, you are more likely to find a good morning-coffee and light-luncheon trade that will yield a fairly steady income all the year round; whereas in a cheaper, more rural setting you may well have to turn away customers, due to a lack of space, at busy holiday times and at weekends, and be far too quiet on ordinary weekdays. The best compromise is a site in a smallish country town, not too far from a larger town or on the way to a well-known beauty spot or seaside resort. Motorists, on the whole, dislike the noisy atmosphere of a commercial café and prefer to seek out somewhere where they can expect to find home cooking, a congenial atmosphere and, perhaps, a cream tea.

When looking for your first tearoom there are two possible alternatives: either you find a new building where you have scope to create your own atmosphere or you purchase a 'going concern'. The latter is not always a cheap proposition - especially if it is freehold with some land and in a good position for the business. The price for such an establishment will include something for the goodwill and most of the capital equipment. Beware of 'goodwill' - it is not a tangible thing and, once a teashop is under new management, existing customers will come to see if they still like it. If for any reason they do not agree with the new ideas that you have put into practice, no amount of money spent on goodwill will make them change their minds! It is your job to make them welcome and make them want to return.

If you do decide to look for a 'going concern', you may find a suitable place advertised in a local newspaper or in such publications as *The Lady*. Alternatively, contact an estate agent capable of dealing with your requirements and state clearly the type of business in which you are most interested, otherwise you may be given details of the wrong type of premises - for example, large hotels or the kind of snack bar which would attract the wrong sort of clientele. When you do receive particulars of properties, be careful to check very thoroughly the information you have been given; estate agents try to promote the properties they are handling and may easily make them sound more desirable than they actually are! I once went to view a property (details of which I had been sent) which was described thus: 'a small picturesque tearoom, practically on the beach'. What I found was a derelict building, in fact a small garage for the promenade bus, which was, of course, very dirty inside and totally unsuited to my purpose. It was obvious that the estate agent involved had not actually visited the building before circulating the details. Luckily not all agents are so careless.

After finding details of a property that interests you and is within your price range, the next step is for you to contact the owner in order to make an appointment to view the premises. (The estate agent handling the property may make these arrangements for you.) Early afternoon is a good time at which to inspect a 'going concern'; the lunchtime trade will have finished and afternoon teas will not yet have begun. It is worth arriving in the town or village during the morning in order to have a good look around - particularly at other tearooms and catering establishments in the neighbourhood. Go into a nearby shop and ask if they can recommend somewhere where you can get a light lunch. They are usually happy to do so, and if it is the place that you have come to view - wonderful! Continue your reconnoitre by having a quick cup of tea or coffee in one of the rival teashops and, while you are there, take particular notice of the type of customer that it attracts and the type of staff employed there. At lunchtime, go to 'your' tearoom and ask if you may have lunch (obviously do not say at this stage who you are). Notice how well you are treated, the number of staff on duty, the number of tables that are reserved and make a mental note of all this information. Make sure, though, that you do not appear too inquisitive. You will also see whether the other customers seem satisfied with their meals and if their comments are complimentary. Having eaten your lunch, leave the premises and mull over all that you have seen and heard, then return at the pre-arranged time for your appointment.

It helps to take along with you a note book, in which you should have already jotted down the questions you want to ask the intending vendor of the tearoom, and remember to make a note in it of all your findings - never trust your memory.

Often ill health is given as the reason for selling a 'going concern', so try to find out what kind of ill health the owner suffers from. Is it caused by unhealthy working conditions, for example, damp? Is it caused by overwork? Or is it through worry because the business is not profitable? If the latter is the case, find out whether the business could carry more staff, particularly if a more extensive menu would mean increased custom.

Obviously, if any of the reasons for the sale of the property worry you, do beware, or you may also find yourself forced to sell sooner than you had intended. But you may, perhaps, find that the owner is a late riser and tends to muddle through the morning-coffee period, making cakes and scones which would be better made well before the teashop opened. This kind of inefficiency and lack of organisation may, in due course, lead to tiredness and ill health. If you have helped in the running of a tearoom before, you will know what to look out for and the kind of questions to ask in order to find out as much as you can before committing yourself.

Always engage the services of a solicitor when embarking on property transactions and never rush into signing a contract, however excited you are. You have a right to know as many details as possible before making an offer, and if you feel that you are having difficulty in getting answers to your questions, it may be better to look elsewhere. It is also essential to seek advice from a chartered accountant. He will be able to advise you as to the real value of the business, whether the tearoom has been run efficiently and whether the books have been kept in the proper manner.

Below is a suggested list of questions that you, as a purchaser, should ask. You can then present the answers to your accountant to obtain advice before you make your final decision.

1. What is the annual rent on the property?
2. What are the annual rates?
3. How long has the lease to run?
4. Can the lease be renewed when it expires? If so, at what price?
5. Is the lease renewed in writing?

6. Is the lease on a graduated scale (some business premises have a lease whereby there is a price rise every, say, three years)?
7. Ask to see the lease for yourself.
8. What are the annual gas, electricity and fuel charges? What rate is charged?
9. How is the water used charged for? Is there a meter?
10. Is there main drainage? If not, is there a charge for clearing the cesspit?

As a prospective purchaser you are entitled to see the audited accounts for the previous trading period, and from these you must find out:

1. What is the average weekly income from meals?
2. What was the annual gross income for the last two years?
3. What are the final gross profits?
4. Have the accounts been audited?
5. What is the weekly wage bill, the number of employees and their hours worked?
6. What is the weekly income from sidelines, such as the sale of gifts?
7. What are the hours of opening, and how many days per week?
8. Does the owner draw a weekly or monthly salary, and how much?

Other things should be noted when inspecting a 'going concern', such as whether the staff are happy, clean and well-trained. You will see the food and the menu. Consider whether or not you would need to make drastic changes. You should also ask when the place was last decorated, both inside and out, and examine the furniture to find out whether it is satisfactory or whether it needs replacing. Look carefully at the kitchen equipment, china, cutlery and glasses to assess how long they will last. Finally, look around to see if you would need to alter anything that would incur additional cost, and check on any outstanding payments.

Prepare a detailed budget and remember that, with inflation, your needs will be considerably greater next year in terms of financial commitment. Make sure you buy somewhere you can comfortably afford. If, after all these things have been considered, you are still very interested, arrange to see it again. You must be absolutely sure that it is the perfect place from which to run a successful business. Have a survey carried out before going ahead.

A house or cottage suitable for conversion into a small teashop will not be cheap to rent or buy, but it may well be less expensive than a purpose-built catering establishment. It will certainly be more fun to furnish, but will involve a lot of hard work. Bear in mind that, on top of the cost of the premises, you will need to purchase a great deal of equipment. If you buy on credit, and a lot of companies specialise in this, ensure that the regular repayments are within your budget. The cheapest way to start this type of venture can be to use your own house if it is in a suitable location. However, you must get permission from your local authority before you start converting a domestic property to commercial use. In fact, it is very unlikely that any property you select will be immediately suitable for use as a tearoom since establishments serving food have to meet certain standards.

It is important that you contact your local authority's Environmental Health Officer. He will inspect the property, discuss the nature of your business, and tell you exactly what is required by law. This information can also be obtained from Her Majesty's Stationery Office and covers working conditions, structure of the building, sanitation, hygiene and such matters as the storage and handling of food, and the health and clothing of people handling food. Ask the local Fire Officer to inspect the building and give his recommendations and advice.

I have always tried to live on the premises in which I have run my tearooms. This arrangement has many advantages - not least the fact that it saves you money! You are able to start work early each morning, and there is no tiring journey home each evening. I also think that your presence will deter any prospective burglar or vandal, since the property will hardly ever be left unattended at weekends or over night. Obviously, you must go into the question of insuring the property and contents. Ask your solicitor for his advice.

When you are searching for a suitable property, try to choose somewhere with a reasonably large frontage; a narrow shop front does not have quite the same attraction as a larger one. In general, prospective tearoom owners look for older-style places with oak beams, perhaps because we have been conditioned to associate rustic architecture with good home cooking. Georgian-style buildings, with bow windows, are also traditional settings for tearooms. Square-shaped rooms are much easier for the service of food than narrow rooms, so bear this in mind. I found that, in a long narrow room, it is not easy to see customers as they arrive and they may be missed by the waitress. This, of course, causes annoyance on both sides.

If you find a property with an attractive garden, then this can become a delightful extension of your tearoom on a hot summer day. Remember, though, that you will have to keep the garden looking tidy and colourful, and that you may also need an extra person to help serve teas outside.

Among the other things to bear in mind when looking for ideal premises is the heating system currently in use. Solid fuel boilers mean extra work in cleaning and refuelling, so that one of the other, more convenient, forms of fuel may be a better choice, and will be cleaner too - an important point to consider on premises where food is prepared. If you intend changing the heating system for any reason, then make sure that you obtain at least three estimates from a selection of reputable local firms who specialise in this; you will be surprised at their variation.

Remember that everything revolves around the kitchen, so make certain that it will be a pleasant place in which to work. The lighting must be adequate; it may even be worth enlarging a window in a dark room. Fluorescent strip lighting should be installed, and each light controlled by a separate switch. Avoid a kitchen where there are steps to different levels or into the tearoom itself. This can be very tiring for your staff and can be an extra hazard to waitresses carrying hot foods on trays. Have the kitchen walls tiled or painted for easier cleaning if they are not already, possibly using a fly repellent paint. Working surfaces ought to be of a laminated material for ease of cleaning and if the floor is brick or stone it should be covered, preferably using a cushioned type of flooring with a non-slip finish. See that there are sufficient shelves all around the kitchen for easy storage; sliding cupboard doors are easier to use than hinged types which can be a hazard if left open. They also save valuable space. Be generous with hooks on the walls from which to hang cups and cooking utensils, instead of having to search for them in drawers and cupboards.

If you anticipate a large sale of home-baked cakes, it may be worthwhile providing a separate kitchen for their preparation. This could act as a service room at lunchtime and in the afternoon for teas, as cake-making ought to have been finished by then.

You will need a separate room, leading from the kitchen, set aside for washing-up, and equipped with plenty of draining space. A large kitchen is not necessary, but a well-planned one is.

Remember, also, to check that there are nearby parking facilities and that there is space for your suppliers to unload their vans.

FURNITURE AND FITMENTS

This is, perhaps, the most exciting part of the business, especially if you are lucky enough to start from scratch and are not taking over colour schemes and furnishings from someone else. If you are, however, using existing decorations and furnishings, a few minor alterations - even the introduction of new curtains of your own choice - can add a touch of your own personality to the place without costing a fortune. After all, when you decided to buy the tearoom, you were presumably attracted to its atmosphere, so it cannot be totally unsuitable!

You alone must choose which style of furniture you wish to buy, whether antique, reproduction or modern, but bear in mind the structure of the room itself in your final choice. If it is uncompromisingly regular in shape, with large picture windows, then modern furniture would, perhaps, suit this room better than an older style. The older 'cottage-style' tearoom is the ideal setting for oak tables and stick-backed chairs with loose, perhaps patterned, cushions.

My own taste tends to be 'old cottage' with round, polished oak tables, wheel-backed chairs and a spotlessly clean, polished floor, preferably in wood. In the winter I like to see an open fire burning in the hearth, and tables lit, if practical, by candles and always a little pot of fresh flowers on each table. Round tables not only, in my opinion, look delightful, but it is easy to make room at them for one extra person when necessary. I dislike the use of tablecloths; they make a room look smaller and after only one minor accident with coffee or food, they need changing. Raffia or wicker table mats are both convenient and practical for use under hot plates, teapots and hot water jugs. They may be washed or wiped clean and, being of neutral colour, blend in well with any colour scheme.

Imagine, if you can, an old room with a low ceiling crossed with oak beams (not so low, though, that tall customers stun themselves!), with plain primrose or magnolia paintwork, and glazed chintz curtains at the old bay window. The curtain material has a lovely deep-crimson background with bunches of geranium leaves, in shades of palest green tinged with brown, as the main design. Below the window is a low shelf on which stands a pair of silver candlesticks supporting tall red candles. These can be lit in the winter months, when the windows are inclined to steam up, in order to give a warm glow to the room. Between the candles stands a large copper jug, in which there is always a fresh arrangement of flowers. At the other end of the room is an old-fashioned fireplace where logs blaze in winter; while in summer a large copper jug or bowl of flowers or, perhaps, some pretty pot plants, stand in the base of the fireplace. On the mantelshelf above more colour is displayed in yet still more pot plants or flowers. There is usually a flower arrangement on each table, or, perhaps, a candle, which can be lit early on dark winter afternoons. The floor gleams, the tables shine and the entire room expresses a welcome to every customer and a promise of delicious home-cooked fare. Such was the arrangement of my own tearoom and few customers failed to remark on the delightful atmosphere that had been created.

When buying tables, whether oak or mahogany, choose ones that will seat four people, but are not too large. In a small tearoom there is little point in offering large tables which take up a lot of floor space, since few people enjoy sharing their table with strangers; most customers prefer a table to themselves or to share with friends.

Plenty of ideas for furnishings may be seen in magazines and in the furniture departments of a large store, for what looks comfortable and welcoming as a domestic scheme will also work in a tearoom.

Lighting is another matter to be considered very carefully, but it is so often overlooked. Lights should be sufficiently bright to enable customers to read the menu and to see what they are eating, but must not be glaring. Centre lights give out too harsh a brightness, so I prefer secondary lighting in the form of wall-mounted lamps. The service area must, of course, be very well lit.

Whatever the style in which you furnish your tearoom, cleanliness is of paramount importance. After each serving period - after serving coffee mid-morning and after lunch and afternoon tea - the floor and tables should be thoroughly cleaned to preserve them in a clean and attractive state, using scented polish as and when necessary. Remember to empty ash trays after each customer, since they can make the room smell stale very quickly.

Finally, you will have to consider whether or not to provide background music in your tearoom. By that I do not mean a loud radio blaring from the kitchen - this will do nothing to enhance the atmosphere. Background music is very much a matter of choice. Personally I dislike it, but to some people it is acceptable, even pleasant. You will also need to consider how you will deal with the smokers among your customers. If there is sufficient room, it would be wise to organise a separate 'smoking' area so as to minimise the discomfort that non-smokers may suffer.

A business may fail for a variety of reasons, which are not always obvious. It may simply be that carelessness when collecting customers' payments and when giving change results in a lower income than anticipated. However, business may fall off for more subtle reasons. A badly kept entrance, such tatty decorations as dusty plastic flowers and badly soiled table linen can disappoint customers; so, too, can dusty corners and dirty ash trays. Bad smells and noises from the kitchen can irritate customers who want a quiet snack or meal and so do chipped china, smeared glasses and badly washed cutlery. If you have a cloakroom, make sure that there is a plentiful supply of soap, toilet rolls and hand towels or roller towel; lack of these facilities can annoy a customer even though he has enjoyed his meal in your tearoom. Remember, too, that all food must be served at its correct temperature - hot food hot and cold food cold. These observations may seem obvious and petty but to disregard them may be to spoil an otherwise good meal. I know, because I ran a tearoom for over twenty years, and realise that these details are worth attending to.

Customers expect good, well-cooked food, attractively presented and quickly and pleasantly served. If they are satisfied and do not feel they have been overcharged, they will return and bring their friends, which is the best kind of advertisement you can have.

THE EQUIPMENT YOU WILL NEED

In a small tearoom seating about forty customers, two cookers ought to be sufficient to allow for each oven to be set at a different temperature, thus allowing for a variety of baking. At the start, when there is so much equipment to be purchased, it is worth considering a roasting oven rather than a cake oven. I found this to be good advice during my last seven years in catering life. Convector ovens are also available and, although perhaps more expensive, are ideal for catering purposes because they cook at the same temperature throughout, thus eliminating the different zones of heat normally found in ovens. Your local gas, electricity or solid fuel showrooms will be able to advise on the types of oven available for catering purposes and their current prices.

You will require a large oven with four shelves for baking cakes and scones, and with five or six shelf positions to allow plenty of scope. Baking trays for the cooking of scones, pastries and biscuits must be about 3 inches (7.5 cm) smaller than the size of the shelves, to allow for the correct circulation of heat around the trays. An oven with a large grill is also preferable, unless a free-standing grill is available, plus at least four burners on each cooker.

A 4-gallon stainless steel urn will provide the boiling water you need for making tea and coffee. A flat lid on an urn makes an ideal spot on which to warm up a covered tin tray of scones. (Scones quickly become dry if kept warm in the oven.)

Coffee may be made in a jug and the jug placed in a large pan of hot water on a hotplate. Cona coffee makers, filter systems and percolators are more expensive alternatives. Take time to consider which method you intend to use. Whichever you choose, use a good brand of coffee, preferably freshly ground. Add milk separately. Not everyone takes their coffee with milk, and if coffee and milk are mixed in advance this affects both the colour and the flavour. Strain hot milk into small jugs or directly into the cups in order to catch any skin that may have formed. Many customers like cream in their coffee and you may choose to serve coffee with cream in your tearoom.

An ice cream conservator is a very useful item of equipment as ice cream is in demand throughout the year in most tearooms. Do not, though, fall into the trap of serving only a choice of ice cream or cheese and biscuits for the lunchtime dessert. However, ice cream ought always to be available and it may, of course, be varied by the addition of a selection of home-made sauces or with fruit as a sundae. Some ice cream manufacturers will happily supply you with a conservator but in return expect you to give them your entire contract for the ice cream you use. Home-made ice cream is delicious and not difficult to make. Always keep a jug of hot water nearby when serving ice cream, so that, after use, the scoops may be placed in the water.

A freezer is, of course, an extremely useful piece of equipment if you are able to afford one. It will enable you to bake large batches of cakes and scones that can then be frozen for future use. You will also be able to store freshly cooked left-overs (provided they have not already been frozen and thawed) for use in another dish on another occasion. More importantly, perhaps, you will be able to buy perishable foods and meats in bulk, so that you benefit from both a saving in cost and from a plentiful supply of ingredients to cope with sudden increases in trade. Remember, when using a freezer, to wrap all items separately and correctly, so that they do not deteriorate and so that flavours from one food will not penetrate another. This also applies to the storage of foods in an ordinary refrigerator. An upright freezer is easier to use than a chest freezer, in which foods are hard to see and may be forgotten. An upright freezer has the added advantage of taking up less floor space. Use foods in strict rotation and check for storage times in the maker's instruction manual or in a reputable freezer cookery book.

You will, of course, require an ordinary refrigerator for the short-term storage of perishable foods, left-overs and dairy products. The brand and size of this will depend very much upon the amount of space you require both in the main body of the refrigerator and in the separate compartment in which salad stuffs may be kept crisp.

You will need a washing-up room or area with two sinks and plenty of draining space. A dishwasher may be an extravagance at first. Ensure that there is always a constant supply of hot water and clean cloths with which to dry cutlery and glass; plates can drain in racks beside the sink. Empty teapots into a large bucket which has a colander dropped in at the top. This is an ideal way to catch tea leaves and tea bags, which quickly smell very unpleasant and should go in a separate dustbin. Coffee grounds can cause blocked drains if washed down the sink, and, of course, they should never be tossed straight into a bin. Train your staff to wrap up garbage before placing it in a dustbin.

On the subject of waste, ensure that you have adequate dustbins available, and place them well away from the kitchen window and tearoom area. Disinfect these regularly and instil in staff the importance of washing their hands after touching the bins. Check with your local authority that the bins are emptied regularly.

Room must be made available in the kitchen for a hand basin which, together with a plentiful supply of disposable hand towels, must be reserved solely for the washing of hands. This basin must be quite separate from the general sink used for the preparation of foodstuffs. It is important that your staff realise the importance of hygiene. Notices in prominent places by the hand basin and in the staff lavatory area stating 'Now wash your hands' should act as a constant reminder. You must provide a good supply of hot water, hand towels and soap. Consult the health regulations.

You will almost certainly require a food mixer, which you will find of invaluable assistance in the making of cakes and pastry. If at all possible, buy the range of attachments which will be available with the mixer you choose, as, again, they will help save time and effort. Personally I find that pastry is a little lighter when mixed by hand, but if you have staff who are at all heavy handed then a mixer attachment is the answer. This applies also to potato mashing and yeast dough making, where mixer attachments are time saving and useful. Remember, however, that you will need to choose a commercial mixer, as a domestic model will not withstand the continual use that you would give it.

You will need somewhere to store cakes - it is impossible to have cake tins stacked in various corners of the kitchen - and a specially designed fitment may be the answer. Ideally you should have installed a cupboard with space for plenty of shelves, with runners so that the shelves may be moved up or down depending on the size of cakes to be stored. Insist that the doors, preferably of the sliding kind, are always kept closed when not in use, to stop the cakes becoming dry and to prevent flies from entering. Space near the top of the cake cabinet is useful so that cake forks and plates, together with cake servers, may be kept always at hand. The shelves of the cupboard, which should be long and narrow for preference, should be made of an easily cleaned material, such as glass, plastic or a laminate.

Apart from those items of equipment already mentioned, the following smaller items will also be necessary for a tearoom which will seat forty customers at one sitting, and where baking is to be done on the premises:

1 free-standing electric mixer, with attachments
hot-water urns
scales with weights, both imperial and metric
selection of china, Pyrex and plastic mixing bowls
cake tins (a 7-in [18-cm] sandwich tin cuts into 6-8 portions; 12 should be sufficient; non-stick)
12 oblong Swiss roll tins (not only for Swiss rolls, but also for flat cakes which are then cut into shapes and iced and for cookies)
4-6 12 in x 16 in (30 cm x 40 cm) slab cake tins
several patty tins, both deep and shallow
2 large mixing bowls for yeast cookery
6 wire cake racks on which to cool cakes and biscuits
1 griddle (for drop scones and potato scones)
2 icing turntables
1 set plain biscuit cutters, 1 set fluted
2 nylon piping bags, plus a selection of nozzles
1 cookie press
1 rolling pin
several wooden spoons of assorted sizes
2 small wooden spatulas
1 rubber or plastic bowl scraper
1 or 2 nylon sieves

2 pastry brushes
1 brush for brushing baking tins with oil
1 chopping board (if you intend preparing lunches you will need 2 more - one on which to chop vegetables and another for raw meat)
1 stock pot (if lunches are to be served)
2 large kettles
2 x 4-pint (2.25-litre) non-stick saucepans
4 small non-stick saucepans
1 large frying pan
1 omelette pan
1 milk saucepan
2 double saucepans to use when preparing icings and fondant and in which to melt chocolate
1 x 2-pint (1-litre) measuring jug
2 x ½-pint (300-ml) pudding basins
6 deep pie plates
selection of large and small jugs for cooking purposes
large and small jars and containers for food storage
1 electric hand whisk
1 upright grater
1 rotary grater
1 nutmeg grater
1 pair kitchen scissors
selection of French kitchen knives (the best you can afford)
1 knife sharpener
1 set cocktail biscuit cutters
1 large strainer
2 small strainers
4 British standard tablespoons

several British standard teaspoons
1 fish slice
1 pancake turner
1 perforated draining spoon
1 cooking fork
1 egg timer
1 set skewers
1 lemon squeezer
1 grapefruit knife
1 flour dredger
1 sugar dredger
1 tea caddy with spoon tied to it
1 large plastic container for sugar
1 butter curler or pat maker
1 egg slicer
1 bean shredder
1 parsley and mint chopper
2 ice cream scoops
You will also need a plentiful supply of greaseproof paper, cling film, aluminium foil and draining paper.

A pop-up toaster, while not strictly necessary, is worth its weight in gold if you intend serving high teas and light lunches. Failing this, a large grill on the cooker will do; its one disadvantage being that it must be watched, whereas a toaster may be left to work itself. It is better to buy a toaster that will take four slices at once - it is amazing how popular hot buttered toast can be at teatime, particularly if one customer sees another eating it!

An egg poacher is also very useful - try to buy one

with a non-stick lining for ease of serving and washing-up.

A large kettle is useful in the morning, when some customers prefer to order tea instead of morning coffee. Teabags are ideal then for single cups of tea, and often a customer only requires one cup, not the pot of tea which is usually served.

You will need sufficient trays of various sizes; melamine ones are good and are easy to clean. Check that the trays you buy are really strong and will not buckle after a few days. You will need about six large trays for teatime use and four small round ones for serving coffee.

Be sure to have a really firm working surface or a solid table in the kitchen. It would be a disaster if a tray of one hundred scones, or, worse still, some newly iced cakes, were to fall on to the floor, just because someone brushed against the leaf of the table.

You will need a small counter for the tearoom and a reliable till in which to store the money you take during the day.

For the tearoom you will require the following items for the service of meals and beverages to forty customers at a time.

teapots 8 x size 1; 16 x size 2; 12 x size 4 - heavy pottery such as Denby, is ideal

hot-water jugs 30 x ½-pint (300-ml) size; 30 x 1-pint (600-ml)

milk jugs 8 x size 1; 16 x size 2; 12 x size 4

sugar bowls 30 should be sufficient

jam dishes 30
tumblers 30 x ½-pint (300-ml); 30 small ones for fruit juice
water jugs 1 for each table and 1 or 2 in reserve
flower vases 1 for each table and 3 in reserve
ash trays 1 for each table and, if they are breakable, 3 in reserve
dinner plates 50 x 10-in (25-cm)
fish plates 50 x 8-in (20-cm)
tea plates 130 x 6-in (15-cm)
soup bowls 30
cups and saucers not less than 130 (these are the most frequently broken items)
fruit dishes or bowls 50
glass sundae or ice cream dishes 50
salt, pepper and mustard pots 1 set for each table
dinner knives 60
cheese knives 60
tea knives 60
dinner forks 60
dessert forks 60
teaspoons 130
fish knives and forks 30 to 40 sets
table mats 60

ENGAGING STAFF AND TEAROOM SERVICE

One of the most important aspects of running a tearoom is the engaging of reliable and happy staff. Once you have done this they will take their tone from the person in charge, whether the manageress or owner.

First of all, contact the Wages Inspectorate for your area. They will advise you on the requirements of the Employment Act and will give you details of the minimum statutory wage for full-time and part-time staff, holiday entitlements, etc. You will be required to keep wage and time records for everyone who works for you and you must also get hold of a copy of the Shop and Premises Act from your local authority. This lists workers' entitlements and should be on display.

Occasionally you may employ a person who turns out to be difficult to work with. If this is the case, you will need to replace her as soon as possible so that other, more reliable, members of staff and, of course, your customers are not upset by her manner. One requires considerable patience when dealing with people, whether they are staff or customers.

However, before you take on staff, it is wise to find out about dismissal procedure. It is not always as easy to fire someone as it is to hire them.

So that you can keep the personal atmosphere which is so important to the success of a small tearoom, it is obviously an advantage to employ as few members of staff as possible, but without overtaxing any one of them, yourself included. It may be tempting to engage fully trained staff, but do not overlook a willing and keen learner. A young, intelligent girl will be quick and eager to learn, and, provided that she has a pleasing manner, will become popular with both staff and customers alike. Some customers even prefer to be served by someone who, though efficient, is not too slick, than to be overawed by the self-assurance of a trained waitress. Do not expect an unqualified member of staff to take on too much of the responsibility or, for that matter, all the most mundane jobs, right from the start; and it is obviously better to put someone with more knowledge of the business in charge of the till.

You will quickly get to know local people and soon find out if anyone is looking for part-time or full-time work. Other ways of recruiting staff are through advertisements in the local newspaper or through a domestic staff agency, if there is one serving the area.

The owner may, in view of the high cost of skilled labour, prefer to do most of the cooking and baking herself, and this is possible if she is prepared to make an early start each day and stick to a fairly rigid timetable. It may be necessary to employ someone, on a part-time basis, just for the busy lunchtime period; he or she can cook the snack meals and prepare salads and sandwiches. If your tearoom seats forty people, you should be able to do the waitressing, with perhaps some additional help over lunch. Be in charge of the till yourself. A busy tearoom of this size will need someone to do the washing up; this job could also include help with coffee and tea-making throughout the day. Whoever has most artistic flair should check that pre-arranged dishes, such as salads and sandwiches, look attractive and have been tastefully garnished before they are served.

Staff like to feel involved with the business, so always be approachable and try to include them and listen to their views when considering any changes. That way, you will gain their loyalty and confidence.

Tips, following the usual custom, are likely to be given to the staff by the customers in recognition of the service they have been given, and it is most practical to suggest that any tips received should be pooled and shared equally by all members of the staff. The person who washes up has a dull and boring job - but, by being allowed to share in the tips, will be far more interested in the work. It is important to get the full co-operation of every member of your staff in the day-to-day running of the place, and to make each one feel that the work he or she is doing is worthwhile and plays a valuable part in the smooth running of the tearoom.

Waitresses must be fully trained in the presentation of bills and, if there is a till near to the door, they must be told at what point in the meal you prefer them to present the bill and to ask the customers to pay on leaving. If money is taken by the waitress, then time must be allowed before the customers are ready to leave for change to be returned to their tables. There can, of course, be much controversy over customers' bills and the appropriate time at which to present them.

I found the following method to be satisfactory, and it also provides a constant check on what has been served to each table.

Use small bill pads, a different colour for each type of meal - for example, pale green bills for morning coffees; white for lunches and pink for teas.

Once a customer has ordered the items he or she requires and they have been served, the waitress should place the bill under the sugar bowl on the table to eliminate the problem, for the customer, of having to catch the waitress's eye in order to ask for the bill. Customers, too, can relax and know that they may leave whenever they are ready to do so.

Using this method, one person is kept in sole charge of the contents of the till, which can be checked each morning and evening by that one person. I have found that problems arise when everyone has access to the till and mistakes are harder to trace when several people are involved. This method is also most acceptable from a hygiene point of view, since nobody is dealing with both food and money at the same time.

I have also found that, by asking customers to pay at a till on leaving the tearoom, there seems to be a quicker turnover of customers, possibly because they decide to leave and get up and go. If waitresses take the money at the tables, customers, while waiting for their change, tend to start another lengthy conversation and so continue sitting long after their change has been given. If customers pay at the till you can, if you like, provide a box for tips there, rather than relying on coins being placed under a saucer on the table.

It is best to make a note of the number of the first bill on each bill pad each morning, to provide, daily, a simple checking system of meals served and monies taken. If a waitress were to destroy the evidence of a bill so that she could 'pocket the money', this checking method would show which bill numbers were missing.

Another matter to be considered is the number of hours you wish to remain open for the service of meals. The location of the tearoom will have some bearing on this. I once had a tearoom situated on the main Southampton-to-Winchester road and had a fairly brisk seasonal trade for breakfasts in the summer, but this is, of course, unusual. Generally, customers tend to come for morning coffees from 10.30 am onwards, so 9.30 am is early enough to open. However, if you happen to be near to a hospital or factory where people are working on a shift system, an earlier start in the mornings may bring in more coffee trade from those wanting an early cup of coffee and a tasty slice of cake or a scone and butter.

Usually it is better to finish serving morning coffees at around noon, so that your space can be taken up, from noon until about 2 pm, by those wanting light lunches. One has to become hard when it comes to business, and it is not worth your while serving coffees during a busy lunchtime period to people just waiting for their bus home, if you are having to turn away customers who would eat a proper meal.

At lunchtime, try plated service; it helps to keep down costs. The food must be arranged attractively to please the eye and stimulate the appetite. Service dishes for vegetables take up a lot of space on a small table.

Personally, I have never liked a self-service system in a tearoom, since people are moving about much more and jostle one another. Things tend to get knocked and spilled more frequently than where there is a waitress system. I always feel that in a self-service establishment there is an air of confusion, whereas a tearoom ought to be a peaceful place. People enjoy being waited on when they go out for morning coffee just as much as the actual drink or food that they consume!

Good organisation is the key to the successful running of a tearoom. Although I am no superwoman, I have, in the past, served one hundred and ten teas to customers, with the help of just one very capable person in the kitchen, between 3.30 pm and 6 pm on a Sunday afternoon. In order to achieve this sort of throughput of customers, you must be well organised 'behind the scenes'. To save time, scones may be cut and buttered and arranged in the cake cupboard, cakes can be sliced into portions and a stack of plates and cutlery placed nearby for quick service of these items. It helps, too, if the sugar basins and milk jugs are kept filled, and jam or honey pots always replenished as necessary.

With the help of your staff, plan a route to which everyone waiting at tables should keep, in order to minimise the distance they walk and to avoid bumping into one another. Arrange items on trays at teatime in a set manner, so that it is easy to spot if something is missing. Make sure, if possible, that tables are cleared by your waitresses as soon as customers have vacated them, and that dirty dishes are taken straight to the washing-up area, ready for the washer-up to take over. This team work is all-important in the smooth running of any business, and particularly where meals are prepared and served.

Your staff, as well as yourself, will require a break for a meal, and it is preferable to close the tearoom for a short time, after the lunchtime rush, whilst you take your meal. Do have a proper meal during this period, as you will get very tired and irritable if you continue working on an empty stomach, and this will not help to achieve that pleasant atmosphere for which you are striving. Make sure that every member of staff is allowed to eat in peace, and do not discuss work. While the staff have their break, open the windows in the tearoom to air the room before the afternoon tea trade begins. If there is time before the tearoom is opened again, clean the floor and check that the tables have been properly laid for teas.

Most tearooms re-open at 3 pm because customers will start coming in at around 3.15 to 3.30 pm. However, as mentioned previously, be flexible here if you need to consider the local workforce. I once owned a tearoom in West Sussex, which, though in the heart of the country, was close to a large hospital. Here, nurses liked to pop in for a cup of tea at about 2.45 pm after their duty and before catching their buses back to work or home; so I used to open in time for them to enjoy their quiet snack. I also, during the summer, would open this tearoom on Sunday afternoons for the service of teas only, whereas during the winter months it was not worthwhile to do so.

However enthusiastic you may be, make sure that you and every member of your staff get time off regularly each week. If you have a business partner this is easier, since you can leave him or her in charge whilst you take your leave, and vice versa. When I was without a partner, I would close the tearoom on Mondays, this being the slack day of the week, and so everyone had time off together. This is, perhaps a better system than not closing at all and having to allow staff to stagger their time off, leaving the others short staffed.

HOW TO PLAN AND COST THE MENUS

The menu planner must study very carefully the type of customer the tearoom attracts and their tastes. It is not possible to lay down hard and fast rules, because there are several matters to be considered - for example, the occupation of your customers, their ages and possible incomes, the time available to them for eating their meals, and so on.

Outdoor country people seem to eat more than town dwellers and those with more money to spend want more choice and the inclusion on the menu of some 'exotic' dishes. I usually found that women tended to eat more salads, fruit, pastry and egg dishes than men and, on the whole, that men eat more than women. There are, of course, exceptions to every rule. These conclusions are not just wild guesses. I ran tearooms in various parts of the country for over twenty years and, during that time, got to know quite a lot about people's likes and dislikes.

Do not try to be too ambitious and include a wider selection of dishes on a menu than is really necessary. Remember that the work entailed in their preparation takes time and, therefore, costs money. Try not to serve the same hackneyed dishes over and over again or you will soon get into a rut. A customer may praise a certain dish, but that does not mean that he or she will want to have it every time they visit your tearoom! If there is a local speciality serve it and also try to serve at least one new dish each week.

One of your aims is to put the customer at his ease and to make him feel he is important, so try to do all you can to please him. One way of doing this is to offer an interesting menu.

You may find it suits your particular clientele if you serve what are known as 'light luncheons', rather than a set three-course meal. Salads and a varied range of sandwiches, hot, cold and toasted, are always popular. Home-made pies, sausage rolls, Welsh rarebit and poached eggs on toast are firm favourites for a light lunch. With these, together with a choice of light desserts, such as mousse, fruit and cream, cheese and biscuits and a selection of ice cream, it is possible to establish a good lunchtime trade.

If you intend serving a set lunch offering no choice, then one menu on the counter is often sufficient. If there is to be a choice, a menu card should be placed on each table, in addition to one outside the door or displayed in the window for potential customers to study.

As I have said before, never be over ambitious. If people want a long, elaborate meal they will surely go to a large hotel or to a high-class, licensed restaurant. Keep your menu simple but interesting and pay as much attention to the balance of food as to the careful seasoning of each dish. Pay attention, also to garnishing dishes attractively - it is so important - but do not allow the food to become cold whilst you fiddle!

In a small tearoom, you could offer a lunch menu on the following lines:

Mushroom Soup
or
Fruit Juice

*

Casserole of Steak and Kidney
Mashed Potatoes
Peas
or
Stuffed Eggs with Green Salad
Crispy Noodles

*

Cherry Pie and Fresh Cream
or
Ice Cream

*

Coffee

And be sure to state the price.

Always give each dish one line to itself; type it, or, if your handwriting is very neat and legible, hand write it. Put the price at the right-hand side of the menu card. You may find it politic to allow people to choose just two courses and not the full set lunch. If so, state the price of each course on the menu separately.

Menu cards can sometimes be obtained free from some of the soft drink manufacturers or the producers of some branded foods. Alternatively, if you prefer plain menu cards, purchase these from a stationer or wholesaler.

Try to have a good selection of cheeses on a board so that the customer can help himself. You will find that few people are greedy, so there is no need to cut off portions beforehand. Remember to serve little butter pats or curls (icy cold) alongside, to go with the biscuits.

Serve as much local produce as possible whenever it is in season; for example, salad stuffs and fresh fruit - particularly local strawberries. They are often cheaper, especially if you collect them yourself.

Always keep some food in store for an emergency. An auction sale in the town may flood your tearoom with extra customers, or a coach load may call in without prior warning. Whenever possible and provided that you have the space, do *not* turn coach parties away. They are usually quickly served and then remove themselves speedily.

A well-balanced meal should contain a good variety of foods - for example: a portion of meat, fish or eggs and a portion of vegetables, followed by some fruit. For most people one type of carbohydrate - such as potatoes, pasta, rice or pastry - is enough. Follow every meal with a drink. Never serve too many foods of the same colour on one plate, or too many creamy dishes in the same meal. A thickened soup before a satisfying meat course is too heavy; far better to begin with fruit juice or a fruit cocktail. Nor is it good to serve the same food more than once in the same meal. You will be able to spot the error made by the planner in this menu: grated cheese on top of onion soup, followed by grated cheese on top of stuffed pancakes, with cheese as the last course!

Few customers want bread rolls or bread at lunchtime, but if you do decide to serve bread, try to provide different varieties, such as wholemeal rolls, granary bread or cottage rolls.

Variety of colour is also very important; we eat with our eyes as well as with our mouths, and do not forget to balance the textures of meals - serve something crunchy as an accompaniment to soft foods.

Try to balance the menu from a cost point of view. There are many foods which may be made to go further, without loss of flavour, such as:

Fish can be made into fish loaf; fish pie; creamed fish in scallop shells; fish pies with pastry topping and fish fritters.

Meat can be served in a casserole with a potato topping; meat cakes; meat balls surrounded by a potato border; hamburgers and chipped potatoes.

Meat pies are popular as well as being economical in their use of left-overs. Serve them individually with vegetables in season.

Fruit can be stretched out in pies, crumbles, trifles and, with a scone topping, as fruit cobbler. You can eke out more expensive, exotic fruits with cheaper seasonal bargains in fruit salad.

Vegetables, particularly broad beans, cauliflower, carrots and leeks, go further when served in a white sauce.

Always have fresh, clean mustard, salt and pepper pots on the tables at lunchtime. Different types of mustard, for instance French or German, are usually appreciated.

You may like to offer your customers a full tea menu, consisting of a pot of tea, scones and cake; alternatively, you can offer a variety of tea menus or serve tea and cakes individually.

Menu costing is a topic which should be carefully studied, either as a pupil on a course or when gaining experience in a tearoom. If prices continue to rise, then your tariff will have to reflect these increases. One point, however, must be borne in mind; never economise on the coffee you serve. The water in various parts of the country does differ enormously, so you should experiment with both coffee and tea to find out which brands are the best suited to your locality.

Never undercharge for food. People do not appreciate it as they may then feel that something may not be up to standard; but, on the other hand, be careful not to price yourself out of business. A small pofit on a dozen meals is preferable to a larger one on one or two customers.

Luncheons are not easy meals to cost, particularly as the price of seasonal ingredients can vary from week to week. Try and work out an average cost per portion and also what you should add as a service charge and contribution towards overheads.

Teas are not such a problem. You know how much each cake has cost you to produce, and into how many portions it will divide. Scones are easy to cost and so are, of course, butter, jam and any extras. Once you have worked out the basic cost of these items, and for tea and milk, again add something as a service charge and towards the cost of overheads. You may sell a number of cakes and scones over the counter, or make cakes to order. It is very important that these, too, are costed carefully.

Overheads consist of:

a) Rent and rates on your premises.
b) Tax and insurance.
c) Interest on the sum spent on capital equipment (list everything bought, then calculate how much this sum would return if it were invested, at current interest rates, in a Building Society, for example).
d) Add 3% of the sum spent on equipment to allow for deterioration and as a fund for renewing and replacing items broken.
e) Total annual amount spent on heating and lighting.
f) Estimate the cost of extras, telephone charges,

stationery, wrapping paper, paper bags, baking cases, aluminium foil and other disposables.

g) Wages for staff and for yourself for the year (remember to include any casual seasonal staff who might be employed for summer periods and bank holidays).

Once you have listed these expenses for the year, divide this sum by twelve, to give an idea of your overheads per month. This sum, divided by the number of working days in an average month, will give you the total daily overheads which must be found, even before a profit is to be made.

If this appears frightening and complicated and you feel that you cannot tackle these costings alone, seek the help of someone who can advise you; preferably enlist the services of an accountant. If, however, you are buying a 'going concern', you have an immediate guide to the yearly expenditure necessary.

One final piece of advice is to visit other tearooms occasionally, so that you can compare prices, portions and value for money.

A GUIDE TO PURCHASING SUPPLIES

Most of the other supplies you will need can, be purchased from a reputable wholesaler; usually there are one or two in the neighbourhood and often they will contact you when you are about to begin trading. If you are not approached by one of the companies, you can find their details in the Yellow Pages or in catering journals, and you can telephone and ask for their representative to call. When he calls, make sure that you spend some time with him; he is an expert in his field and can be one of your most useful contacts. The company will want to rely on your repeat orders and will thus want to ensure that you are happy with the goods you have ordered as a trial. It is a good idea to establish a monthly account with a local greengrocer for all items of fresh fruit and vegetables, and, perhaps, with a local small grocer too. It pays to become known locally by other tradesmen since, when there is a shortage of one commodity, they will usually try to supply you even if it is only with a small amount of whatever you require. This sort of goodwill is extremely helpful to you. You would also be wise to purchase fresh meat, fish and dairy produce locally. Coffee, tea, preserves, canned and frozen foods should be obtained in bulk from your wholesaler, along with flour, dry fruit, sugar and nuts.

It is helpful to keep a well-stocked store cupboard and try to use every item in strict rotation. Careful stocktaking should be carried out regularly, say on a monthly basis. A rule to remember is that careful buying is the road to success; and, as with most occupations, experience will tell you how often to buy and in what quantities.

Here are a few tips, relevant to some of the foods you will require:

Dried fruits - normally sold in 14 lb (6 kg) boxes. Once opened, the fruit is best stored in large polythene containers, with tight-fitting lids, and each type of fruit labelled accordingly. Glass jars also make good containers for dried fruit. Store in a cool, dry place.

Glacé cherries - probably it will be best to buy in smaller quantities, say 11 lb packs (5 kg), since they become hard when kept for too long, and are too expensive to waste. Again, once they are opened, they ought to be stored in an airtight container in a cool, dry place.

Crystallised ginger and pineapple cubes - these are available in 4 lb (1.75 kg) boxes, and are useful for cakes and as cake decorations. Store as for glacé cherries, and use fairly quickly, since they also become hard if kept too long.

Nuts are best purchased in 7 lb (3 kg) packs, and it saves time if shelled nuts are bought. It is probably best to order halved walnuts, chopped mixed nuts, blanched almonds and, if marzipan is used in cakes, ground almonds. Hazelnuts can be used for cake decoration. Store as for dried fruits.

Glycerine - used in many cakes to keep them moist, for example, in fruit cakes. It also has the advantage of making cakes lighter in texture and increasing the yield of the mixture. For fruit and Madeira cakes, use in the proportion of 2-3 oz (50-75 g) to each 1½ lb (750 g) of mixture. It is usually added after the sugar, along with the beaten eggs. It is useful, too, for keeping royal icing on celebration cakes soft and pliable. Store in the bottles in which it is bought.

Eggs - best bought locally, preferably from a reputable farm, in trays which hold two and a half dozen each. Some farms sell cracked eggs slightly cheaper, and, for tearoom use, these are quite satisfactory, since large quantities of eggs are not only used in baking but also for lunches in omelettes, scrambled and poached eggs. Store in a cool, dry place; it is not necessary to refrigerate them, unless they are to be used for meringue mixtures. For baking, it is preferable to have eggs at room temperature so that they do not curdle the mixture when added. Store them with their rounded end uppermost, and away from strong smelling foods, since flavours can be transmitted through their porous shells. Do not buy too many at a time: it is best to buy them frequently, so that they are always fresh.

Flour - usually purchased from a wholesaler, in sacks, but buy from a local miller if at all possible. The sacks must be stored in a cool, dry place, well off the ground on special wooden racks. Buy strong flour for bread-making and soft flour for cakes, biscuits and pies. There is a tendency towards the use of wholemeal flour in baked products today, so it may be worth making some of your pies, scones, biscuits and, of course, bread with either all wholemeal flour or a mixture of half white and half wholemeal. It gives items a particularly 'nutty' flavour. Flour should normally keep for about one month; wholemeal flour ought to be used quicker than white, since it contains a small amount of fat, which can turn rancid if kept for too long.

Jams and preserves - perhaps you will be able to make your own jams from fruits bought locally when in season. This can be another item to sell over the counter to your customers. If you intend to buy jams and preserves choose well-known brands, not necessarily the cheapest, since cheap jam is primarily intended for use in cakes and is not good enough to serve on toast and scones. You may be able to encourage a local jam maker to supply you with her own home-made jam. Local honey, if it is available, is another item which will be popular with customers, and, again, can be sold over the counter in attractive jars or pots.

Essences, fondant and couverture - usually these items can be purchased from your wholesaler, who will advise on the best way to buy them for your use. Store as for dried fruits.

Sugar - you will probably need caster sugar for cake-making, icing sugar for icings and butter-creams, granulated for table use and for cooking fruit etc and demerara or coffee sugar for table use. Store all types as for dried fruits, and be sure to label each kind clearly. You may, of course, consider using cube sugar for tea-table use. Sugar, together with syrup and treacle, should be bought in bulk. If you should run out of caster sugar, granulated sugar may be ground down in a blender for cake-making, and caster may be ground to make an emergency icing sugar.

Tea and coffee - possibly the two most important commodities you will buy for the tearoom. Choose brands carefully, and experiment with different ones until you are really satisfied with the taste. Different water in different areas can affect the flavour of beverages, so be advised by your wholesaler as to the most popular brands of tea and coffee for the area concerned. It is a good idea to stock both Indian and China tea, as some customers do have clear preferences. As a guide, 1 lb (500 g) tea is sufficient for about eighty single teapots, or the same weight of teabags will make about one hundred and twelve single cups of tea. For your costings, allow two cubes or teaspoons of sugar per customer and three teaspoons (15 ml) milk per person; from that, you can work out the unit cost per cup or pot of tea.

Butter and margarine - butter should be served with hot toast, scones, etc. Try to buy the best quality, but make sure it is not too salty. Buy this locally from your grocer or direct from a farm, if at all possible. There are different margarines for different uses. Softer margarines are ideal for cake-making and for sandwiches - hard margarine is more suitable for pastry - both margarines, together with lard, can be bought from your wholesaler. Store all fats (not oils, though) in a refrigerator at about 40°F (4°C). If your refrigerator has a compartment in the door where fats may be stored, use this, since it is the correct temperature. Remember to take fats out of the refrigerator before they are required in order to soften them slightly and make them easier to use.

Bread - if possible, purchase daily from a local baker unless you intend making your own. Use the minimum of sliced bread (for sandwiches only) as it is far nicer to serve freshly cut bread with dishes, or as toast. Bread stores well in a freezer, so an emergency supply can always be kept, but remember to use it in strict rotation. Crusty and soft rolls are also delicious served with such dishes as salads.

A guide to portion control - this table will help you to gauge the amount of stock you need to hold.

Item	*Imperial weight*	*Metric weight*	*Number of servings*
Apples	1 lb	500 g	4-6
Apricots	1 lb	500 g	6
Asparagus	1 bunch	1 bunch	4-5
Bacon (back)	1 lb	500 g	16-20 rashers
Bananas	1 lb	500 g	3-4
Beans (canned)	1 lb	500 g	4-5
Beans (green)	1 lb	500 g	5
Brussels sprouts	1 lb	500 g	4-5
Butter	1 lb	500 g	spreads 3 large loaves
Cabbage	1 lb	500 g	4
Carrots	1 lb	500 g	4-6
Cauliflower	1 lb	500 g	3-4
Chicken meat	1 lb	500 g	3-4
Chicken on bone	3 lb	1.5 kg	4-6
Coffee (ground)	1 lb	500 g	45-48 cups
Cream (whipped)	½ pint	300 ml	16 whirls
Fish (filleted)	1 lb	500 g	4
Fish (on bone)	6 oz	175 g	1
French dressing	½ pint	300 ml	8-10
Ham (sliced)	1 lb	500 g	4
Ice cream	1 pint	600 ml	8
Lemon juice	2 tbs	30 ml	1 lemon
Marrow	1 lb	500 g	4
Meat (cubed)	1 lb	500 g	4-5

Item	*Imperial weight*	*Metric weight*	*Number of servings*
Meat (minced) and offal	1 lb	500 g	5
Mushrooms	1 lb	500 g	5-6
Parsnips	1 lb	500 g	4-5
Peaches (fresh)	1 lb	500 g	3-5 peaches
Pears (fresh)	1 lb	500 g	3-5 pears
Peas (in pods)	1 lb	500 g	2-3
Peppers	1 lb	500 g	6-7
Salmon, tuna, etc (canned)	1 lb	500 g	4-5
Spinach	1 lb	500 g	2
Tomatoes	1 lb	500 g	5

Remember that macaroni, noodles, etc double in volume when cooked, so always allow for this. Rice increases its volume four-fold during cooking.

BOOK-KEEPING

Book-keeping may frighten some people, but, in order to run a tearoom profitably, a certain amount has to be done. Accounts are the only way to keep abreast with the state of the business, and are necessary for tax purposes.

Your first priority must be to seek the help of a chartered accountant who will take care of the preparation of your Annual Financial Accounts and deal with other financial matters for you. He will advise you how your Accounts should be kept, how he would like you to present the information to him, and how you should deal with such things as value-added-tax. It should not be necessary to have an elaborate system, as long as the records are regularly and accurately kept. It is essential that nothing is forgotten or omitted.

Money, unless it is carefully accounted for, can so easily be 'lost', which impresses neither your accountant, the Inspector of Taxes, nor the VAT Inspectors. Bear in mind, also, that you may eventually wish to sell your business in order to move to another location. Prospective purchasers will want to see your Accounts in order to determine the profitability of your business.

Your accountant will probably suggest that you keep the following books. It is a sensible practice to enter the accounts regularly and systematically, and any bills which require payment by you should be dealt with regularly, too. Your bank manager will arrange a business bank account, cheque book and monthly statements. Reconcile your cash book with your bank statements monthly to check your true position and to rectify any mistakes should they have occurred.

Petty cash book - this is a record of all transactions involving cash. On the debit or left-hand side enter cash drawn from the bank and cash received from customers. On the credit or right-hand side enter all cash expenditure and cash paid into the bank. If you are in the habit of making cash payments for small items from the till during the course of each day, it is worthwhile having a notebook in the till in which you can record these transactions.

Cash book - this is a record of all transactions made through the bank. On the debit or left-hand side enter all the money paid into your bank account. On the credit or right-hand side enter all your expenditure: payments by cheque or by standing order, and transfers and bank charges.

Wages book - you are required to keep a record of the hours worked by all members of your staff and, of course, a wages book. You will be responsible for deducting income tax and national insurance contributions; tax deduction cards are available from your local tax office.

You will need to keep a record of your own drawings. These will not be taxed weekly but are taxable twice a year, on January 1 and July 1, under Schedule D.

Order book - in a small tearoom it is not necessary to keep a large order book or purchase ledger. A book in which you keep a duplicate copy of the order is sufficient. Do stress to members of staff who have the authority to order goods that nothing may be ordered without a written record of it in the order book. A detailed invoice will normally be sent with the goods and, when this is received, mark your duplicate copy with the relevant price of each item. Once the invoice is paid, it is entered in the cash book (if paid by cheque) or in the petty cash book (if paid by cash). Note the date of payment on the invoice and on the duplicate copy of the order. The order book should be clearly laid out to give the *date* of the order, the name and address of the *supplier* and your name and address. There should be columns for *quantity* and for *description of goods* ordered. A third column should give the *price*, when known. At the bottom of the duplicate copy only should appear the words *date paid.*

SELLING GIFTS AND OTHER SIDE-LINES

In a small tearoom it is often advisable to have other side-lines in the form of gifts or home-made produce for sale. Morning coffees, light lunches and teas may not alone bring in sufficient income to make a reasonable profit. In addition to the financial profit accruing, items for sale in your tearoom can serve as decoration and create a homely atmosphere for your customers.

If your tearoom is situated in a picturesque spot or is itself particularly attractive, it is worth selling some picture postcards, which can also act as an advertisement for your business. Your local photographer will help with details about pictures for postcards, or you may be approached by postcard manufacturers, particularly if you happen to be in a tourist area. Do, before the order is printed, ask to see a proof copy of the postcard you choose, as alterations are expensive to make. Always check that a representative of a postcard firm does work for whom he says he does!

Small toys may also sell well, especially as Christmas approaches. Hand-made ones are more appealing than cheap manufactured items and you may be able to buy items from a local hand-knitter or someone who does a lot of sewing. Small items of jewellery, particularly if local semi-precious stones are used, might sell well. Try to keep up to date with current fashion trends, as you may be able to sell small articles which are in fashion and make extra income from them. When buying in items for sale always start with a small order - you can always increase it next time. If the items do not sell well, your supplier may not want to take them back. It might be advisable to sell on a commission basis.

You may find that there is an Institute for the Blind in your locality or a local potter who produces household items. The baskets and raffia items made by blind people are popular because, besides being attractive in themselves, they help a worthy cause. Wooden articles, such as candlesticks and napkin rings, are easy to handle, being unbreakable, and are always popular. Local groups, such as the Women's Institute, can often suggest local people who make very attractive items which you could sell. Once local craftsmen and artists know of your interest in selling their work, you will probably be approached by them.

Do make sure that your original idea of running a tearoom is not lost to that of a gift shop. Only sell small items, or you will have to forfeit space for their display.

Cakes, jams, biscuits, sweets and chocolates could also be made by you, packed in pretty containers and sold. Sweets must be weighed on Governmentstamped scales in the shop or tearoom. Bread and scones may also be sold over the counter. Everything should look home-made and wholesome and be attractively displayed in the window or on the counter near the till, always protected by glass or Perspex. These items do make good profits.

Another obvious side-line to your business is that of catering for functions. These may include wedding receptions; cheese and wine parties for local organisations; children's parties; and functions organised by local firms or sports clubs. You have the facilities for this type of business and, provided you are able to spend the necessary time, they can be very profitable and fun to do. From late October to early December business in most tearooms is fairly slack and this is the time to take orders for Christmas cakes and birthday cakes - but only if you are proficient at icing and cake decorating.

BEFORE YOU BEGIN TO COOK

Most of the recipes in the following sections are based on quantities sufficient for twenty, unless otherwise stated. Twenty seems to be a good basis from which to multiply up as required. The servings stated are only approximate, since people's appetites do vary enormously and you will, or course, work out your own portion and costing policy.

In the recipes, both imperial and metric measurements have been given. It must be remembered that the metric quantities are not exact conversions, since these would be hard to weigh out, but they are rounded up to give easier working measurements. **It is important to keep to one method of measurement only, so if you begin by weighing in imperial measurement, then stick to it throughout the whole recipe, and likewise with metric weights.**

Oven Temperatures

	Farenheit	*Centigrade*	*Gas mark*
Very cool	225	110	¼
Cool	250	130	½
	275	140	1
Warm	300	150	2
Moderate	325	170	3

	Farenheit	*Centigrade*	*Gas mark*
	350	180	4
Moderately	375	190	5
hot	400	200	6
Hot	425	220	7
	450	230	8
Very hot	475	240	9

Equivalents of Imperial and Metric weights

Imperial	*Metric*
½ oz	15 g
1 oz	25 g
1½ oz	40 g
2 oz	50 g
3 oz	75 g
4 oz	100 g
6 oz	175 g
8 oz	225 g
10 oz	275 g
12 oz	350 g
1 lb	500 g
1½ lb	750 g
2 lb	1 kg
2½ lb	1.25 kg

Liquid measurements

Imperial	*Metric*
¼ pint (5 fl oz)	150 ml
½ pint (10 fl oz)	300 ml
¾ pint (15 fl oz)	450 ml
1 pint (20 fl oz)	600 ml

Imperial	*Metric*
1½ pints	900 ml
1¾ pints	1 litre
3½ pints	2 litres

Spoon measures

1 teaspoon	5 ml
1 tablespoon	15 ml
4 tablespoons	60 ml
6 tablespoons	90 ml
8 tablespoons (¼ pint)	150 ml

Linear measurements

Imperial	*Metric*
⅛ inch	3 mm
¼ inch	5 mm
½ inch	1 cm
1 inch	2.5 cm
2 inch	5 cm
3 inch	7.5 cm
4 inch	10 cm
5 inch	13 cm
6 inch	15 cm
7 inch	18 cm
8 inch	20 cm
9 inch	23 cm
10 inch	25 cm
11 inch	28 cm
12 inch	30 cm

HOME-MADE SOUPS

The importance of serving a good soup cannot be overstated. If you establish a reputation for good, home-made soups you are halfway to success. Start with a good basic stock. Make this in the evening when the tearoom is closed; the smell will be gone by morning.

Basic Stock

4 lb/2 kg beef bones
4 pints/2.25 litres cold water
2 teaspoons/2 x 5 ml spoons salt

Place the washed bones and water in a large pan or stock pot. Leave to soak for about 1 hour.

Add the salt, cover the pan, then bring slowly to boiling point, reduce the heat, then simmer for about 3 hours.

Carefully remove the scum from the surface of the stock, using a perforated draining spoon.

Strain the stock, through a fine strainer, into a large lidded container. Cool rapidly, then store the stock in a refrigerator.

Basic Cream Soup

8 oz/225 g butter or margarine
6 tablespoons/6 x 15 ml spoons onion, grated
6 oz/175 g plain flour
salt and pepper
6 pints/3.5 litres milk
4 pints/2.25 litres white stock

Place the butter or margarine in a large saucepan, add the grated onion and fry gently, until it becomes clear. Gradually stir in the flour, salt and pepper.

Cook this mixture over a gentle heat, stirring constantly, for about 1 minute.

Gradually blend in the milk and stock. Return the pan to the heat and bring slowly to the boil, stirring constantly. Beat the soup, as it boils, for about 2 minutes.

Serve the soup piping hot.

Serves 24

Note: This is a good basic recipe from which to make a variety of delicious cream soups. White stock may be made from chicken or turkey bones to give a pale colour and light flavour to the stock. Always use white pepper for cream soups and white sauces.

Cream of Chicken Soup

4 oz/100 g chicken fat or butter
6 oz/175 g plain flour
5 pints/2.75 litres chicken stock
5 pints/2.75 litres milk
1½ lb/750 g cooked chicken pieces, cut into small cubes
salt and pepper
chopped parsley or chervil

Place the chicken fat or butter in a large saucepan, allow it to melt, then stir in the flour.

Cook this over a gentle heat, stirring constantly, for 1 minute. Blend in the stock and milk, gradually.

Return the pan to the heat, add the chicken pieces, and bring the soup to the boil, stirring constantly.

Allow the soup to boil for about 5 minutes, then serve, piping hot, sprinkled with chopped parsley or chervil.

Serves 24

Note: This is an ideal way of using up left-over pieces of chicken meat. A little chicken meat goes a long way in this recipe!

Cottage Broth

1 rabbit, skinned, cleaned and quartered
12 pints/6.75 litres water
salt and pepper
6 oz/175 g flour
3 bay leaves
4 oz/100 g parsley, chopped
2 lb/1 kg peas, fresh, frozen or canned
1 lb/500 g carrots, diced
2 round lettuces, shredded finely
8 oz/225 g pearl barley

Place the rabbit pieces in a large saucepan and pour in 4 pints/2.25 litres of the water, and add salt and pepper. Bring to the boil, reduce the heat and simmer with a lid on the pan, for about 1 hour, or until the flesh is tender.

Drain the rabbit pieces, and reserve this stock. Remove the flesh from the bones, and cut into small pieces.

Blend the remaining water carefully into the flour, add the bay leaves, parsley, peas, carrots, shredded lettuce and pearl barley. Gradually stir in the stock, add the rabbit pieces.

Return the pan to the heat and, stirring constantly, bring the soup to the boil. Season, if necessary, with more salt and pepper. Simmer the soup for about 30 minutes, or until all the ingredients are thoroughly cooked. Serve piping hot.
Serves 30

Fish Chowder

2 lb/1 kg white fish, e.g. coley, cod, monkfish, haddock or whiting
3 pints/1.75 litres cold water
3 bay leaves
salt and cayenne pepper
4 oz/100 g streaky bacon, chopped
1½ lb/750 g potatoes, thinly sliced
5 large onions, finely chopped
½ pint/300 ml warm water
8 pints/4.5 litres milk
chopped parsley

Roughly chop the skinned fish, and place it in a large saucepan with the cold water. Add the bay leaves, salt and pepper. Bring to the boil, then cover the pan and simmer for about 10 minutes. Drain the fish and reserve the liquor.

Sauté the bacon in a clean pan, add the potato slices, chopped onion and fish pieces. Cook together for about 5 minutes over a gentle heat.

Gradually blend in the warm water, fish stock and milk. Bring to the boil, then, stirring constantly, simmer for 10 to 15 minutes, or until the flavours have developed. Serve piping hot, sprinkled with chopped parsley.
Serves 30

Note: A fish chowder can make an excellent alternative to meat and vegetable soups.

Mixed Vegetable Soup

8 oz/225 g margarine
8 oz/225 g onions, finely chopped
12 oz/350 g carrots, finely sliced
8 oz/225 g celery, finely chopped
5 large potatoes, finely diced
12 oz/350 g small white turnips, sliced
10 pints/5.5 litres water
4 oz/100 g butter
4 oz/100 g flour
1 lb/500 g tomatoes, skinned and chopped
6 cubes vegetable extract
2 tablespoons/2 x 15 ml spoons brown sugar
1 tablespoon/1 x 15 ml spoon salt
2 teaspoons/2 x 5 ml spoons paprika
chopped parsley

Place the margarine in a large saucepan, add the onions, and sauté for a few minutes, until they are clear. Stir in the carrots, celery, potatoes and turnips. Add the water and bring to the boil. Cover and simmer gently for 1 hour.

Melt the butter in another pan, stir in the flour and cook for 1 minute, stirring constantly.

Add this mixture, a little at a time, to the soup pan, stir in the tomatoes, vegetable extract cubes, sugar, salt and pepper. Reheat the soup, and boil for 1 minute. Serve piping hot, sprinkled with a little chopped parsley.

Serves 24

Green Pea Soup

3 large round lettuces, shredded
5 medium onions, finely chopped
16 pints/9 litres stock (ham stock is delicious)
1 head celery, finely chopped
½ oz/15 g parsley sprigs
5 lb/2.25 kg green peas in their pods
8 oz/225 g butter or margarine
salt and pepper

Place the shredded lettuce, chopped onion and stock in a large saucepan, stir in the chopped celery and parsley. Shell the peas and add the pods to the saucepan. Bring to the boil, cover and simmer for about 20 minutes, or until the ingredients are tender.

Either sieve the ingredients or place in a blender and make into a purée.

Cook the peas in salted boiling water for about 10 minutes, or until tender. Drain and add them to the purée.

Place the soup in a clean saucepan and slowly bring to the boil. Beat in the butter or margarine, salt and pepper. Boil for a few minutes, then serve piping hot.
Serves 40

Note: Delicious served sprinkled with a few croûtons.

Mushroom Soup

4 tablespoons/4 x 15 ml spoons pork or bacon fat
10 oz/275 g spring onions, chopped
2 lb/1 kg button mushrooms, finely chopped
2 cloves garlic, crushed
14 pints/8 litres white stock or milk
salt and pepper

Place the pork fat in a large saucepan and fry the spring onions and mushrooms until soft. Add the crushed garlic and fry briskly.

Stir in the stock or milk (or a mixture of both), salt and pepper. Bring to the boil.

Serve piping hot.

Serves 36

Note: If a thickened soup is required, a little cornflour, blended with a little cold milk, may be stirred into the soup just before serving.

If you decide to serve powdered mushroom soup, try adding a few chopped fresh mushrooms to the soup just before serving, to make it taste more authentic.

Tomato Soup

2 rashers streaky bacon, finely chopped
2 medium onions, chopped
16 pints/9 litres vegetable stock
4 oz/100 g sago
3 lb/1.5 kg ripe tomatoes, or drained
canned tomatoes
6 oz/175 g celery, chopped finely
2 tablespoons/2 x 15 ml spoons sugar
4 pieces thyme
salt and pepper

Place the bacon and chopped onion in a large saucepan; fry together until soft but not brown.

Stir in the stock, sago, tomatoes, celery, sugar, thyme, salt and pepper. Bring to the boil, then cover and simmer gently for 1 hour.

Remove the thyme sprigs from the soup, and serve the soup piping hot.

Serves 40

Note: For a special occasion, pour a whirl of single cream onto the surface of each portion of soup just as it is served.

Emergency Soups

In an emergency, blend together a mixture of powdered soups to give a different flavour to an otherwise convenience soup. For example, mushroom soup and cream of spinach; cream of tomato and cream of celery; cream of chicken and cream of mushroom; oxtail soup and tomato soup.

Some Soup Garnishes

Croûtons – cut stale bread into ¼ inch/5 mm dice. Dip the cubes of bread into hot fat and dry off under the grill, or deep fry and drain. Scatter on the soup immediately before serving.

Kernals - fry puffed-wheat breakfast cereal in hot dripping or lard. These puff up and become crispy. Serve with the hot soup, not floating in it.

Grated cheese - try adding to celery, vegetable and tomato soup before serving.

Sausage drops - stir together, in a large bowl, 1½ lb/750 g pork sausage meat, 2 egg whites, 2 oz/50 g chopped parsley, 1 teaspoon/1 x 5 ml spoon dried basil, 10 oz/275 g brown bread-crumbs and salt. Form the mixture into small balls, drop these into a pan of hot soup and cook in the soup for the last 10 minutes of cooking time. Serve two or three small sausage drops in each portion of soup.

FISH DISHES

The following fish dishes are popular because of their rather unusual nature.

Tuna Fish Balls

4 x 7-oz/200-g cans tuna fish
6 oz/175 g onion, minced
2 oz/50 g parsley, chopped
3 lb/1.5 kg mashed potato
1 small jar stuffed olives, drained and chopped roughly
1 small jar pickled capers, drained
deep fat or oil for frying

Mix together in a large bowl, the flaked tuna fish, onion, parsley, potato, salt and pepper, and chopped olives and capers. Mix thoroughly, then form into small balls. Allow these to set slightly, then lift them into a pan of hot deep fat or oil and fry until golden.

Serve hot, with salad.

Serves 20

Crumb Baked Fillets

5 lb/2.25 kg coley fillets or haddock, plaice or whiting
3 eggs, beaten
8 oz/225 g cornflakes, crushed
1 oz/25 g dried tarragon
salt and pepper
6 oz/175 g margarine
parsley

Cut the fish fillets into 20 equal-sized pieces.

Place the beaten eggs in a shallow dish.

Mix together the cornflake crumbs, tarragon, salt and pepper.

Coat the fish portions first in beaten egg, then dip each into the crumbs so that they are thoroughly covered. Allow to become dry.

Grease shallow baking trays with margarine, allowing a good covering on each, and arrange the fish portions on the trays.

Bake in the centre of a moderately hot oven mark 5, 375°F/190°C, for 15 to 20 minutes.

Serve hot, garnished with a little parsley, and with horseradish sauce or tomato sauce. Delicious served with potato crisps or chipped potatoes and peas or tomatoes.

Serves 20

Hake with Horseradish Sauce

20 hake cutlets
6 oz/175 g butter
6 oz/175 g flour
3 pints/1.75 litres milk
6 oz/175 g prepared horseradish
salt and pepper
paprika

Poach the hake cutlets in shallow, simmering water for about 10 minutes. Drain thoroughly and keep hot. Discard the water.

Melt the butter in a large saucepan, stir in the flour. Stir over a gentle heat for 1 minute, then gradually stir in the milk. Return to the heat and bring to the boil, stirring constantly, then cook for 1 minute. Add salt and pepper.

Add the grated horseradish, then pour this sauce over the cooked hake cutlets, arranged on a shallow oval dish. Sprinkle with paprika.

Serve hot, with vegetables in season.
Serves 20

Note: Other kinds of white fish may be used. This dish needs to be served with a colourful vegetable.

Quick Fish Loaf

4 lb/1.75 kg cooked white fish
5 eggs, beaten
2½ large cans condensed milk
6-8 oz/175-225 g fresh white breadcrumbs
salt and pepper
1½ tablespoons/1½ x 15 ml spoons soy sauce
3 tablespoons/3 x 15 ml spoons margarine, melted
4 oz/100 g parsley, chopped
5 oz/150 g celery, chopped
1 large onion, chopped
2 green peppers, chopped

Flake the fish, then blend in the beaten eggs, condensed milk, breadcrumbs, salt and pepper. Add the soy sauce, melted margarine, chopped parsley, celery, onion and peppers.

Grease loaf tins thoroughly, then divide the mixture between them.

Bake in the centre of a moderately hot oven, mark 6, 400°F/200°C, for 30 minutes.

Serve this fish loaf hot with vegetables in season, or cold and sliced with salad.
Serves 16

Stuffed Fresh Herrings

20 fresh herrings (small mackerel may be used instead)
4 tablespoons/4 x 15 ml spoons vinegar
¾ large sandwich loaf made into crumbs
4 oz/100 g parsley, chopped
6 tablespoons/6 x 15 ml spoons olive oil
salt and pepper

Slit open the herrings and thoroughly clean them. Remove the heads. Sprinkle with a little of the vinegar.

Mix together in a large bowl the breadcrumbs, parsley, remaining vinegar, olive oil, salt and pepper. If necessary, add a little water to make a moist stuffing.

Divide this between the herrings, fold over and fasten each, if necessary, with a wooden cocktail stick.

Grease shallow ovenproof dishes or tins and lay the herrings in these.

Bake in the centre of a moderate oven, mark 4, 350°F/180°C, for 15 minutes. Remove from the oven and grill to make the skins crispy and a golden brown colour.

Serve hot or cold.

Serves 20

Salmon Loaf

1 lb/500 g potato crisps, crushed
3 x 1-lb/500-g cans pink or red salmon
2 lb/1 kg cooked white fish
3 cans condensed mushroom soup
½ pint/300 ml water

Mix together, in a large bowl, the potato crisps, flaked salmon, flaked white fish, soup and the water. Blend thoroughly together.

Grease loaf tins well and divide this mixture between them. Cover with greased greaseproof paper.

Bake in a moderate oven, mark 3, 325°F/170°C, for 1 hour or until firm.

Serve hot or cold, cut into slices, with vegetables in season or a tossed green salad.
Serves 24

Individual Crusty Fish Pies

20 cooked individual pastry shells
4 x 7-oz/200-g cans tuna fish
2 pints/1.2 litres white sauce (page 144)
3 tablespoons/3 x 15 ml spoons dry sherry
1 tablespoon/1 x 15 ml spoon Worcestershire sauce
parsley

Make up and bake the pastry shells, allow to cool.

Flake the tuna fish, removing any bones and skin, and blend in the white binding sauce, dry sherry and Worcestershire sauce. Divide the mixture between the pastry shells. Place these on a baking tray.

Bake in a moderately hot oven, mark 5, 375°F/190°C, for 10 minutes, to heat through.

Serve hot, garnished with sprigs of parsley.
Serves 20

Note: Other fish, provided that it is canned or cooked, is delicious in these pies. Kipper fillets are particularly good, and so, too, are smoked haddock fillets. Tuna fish in these fish pies has a particularly subtle flavour.

Fish Puddings

4 lb/2 kg cooked or canned fish
8 oz/225 g margarine, melted
1 lb/500 g fresh breadcrumbs
6 eggs, separated
4 tablespoons/4 x 15 ml spoons Worcestershire sauce

Blend together the fish, melted margarine and breadcrumbs, then add the beaten egg yolks.

Whip the egg whites in a large bowl until light and frothy, then very carefully fold into the fish mixture.

Grease 20 small individual ovenproof dishes or moulds, and spoon the mixture into each so that the dishes are three-quarters full. Cover with aluminium foil, and steam for 1 hour.

Serve piping hot, with tomato sauce or with a well-flavoured white sauce (page 143).

Serves 20

EGG DISHES

Eggs provide a variety of cheap, interesting and nourishing dishes. It is a good idea always to have some hard-boiled eggs available; they store in the refrigerator for up to three days and may be used for a variety of dishes and as an instant garnish. Ideas are sure to spring to mind, but here are a few simple recipes using eggs.

Poached Eggs

Use an egg poacher in which there are 4 cavities for the eggs, or a shallow saucepan or frying pan. To poach eggs by this second method, half fill the pan with boiling, salted water and add a knob of butter.

Carefully pour the eggs, one at a time, into the gently simmering water, and slowly poach the eggs until they are soft and set sufficiently.

Carefully lift each egg from the water, allow to drain (this is best done by using a slotted spoon), and serve on a slice of hot buttered toast.

Note: Poached eggs make a quick and popular snack. They are delicious served with a coating of thick cheese sauce on top.

Scrambled Eggs

3 large eggs
pinch of salt
pinch of cayenne pepper
3 tablespoons/3 x 15 ml spoons hot water
1 tablespoon/1 x 15 ml spoon melted butter

Beat the eggs thoroughly together in a basin, then add salt, pepper and water. Melt the butter in a small saucepan (preferably a non-stick saucepan).

Pour the egg mixture into the pan, and, stirring constantly, cook the eggs slowly until the mixture thickens slightly. Remove from the heat before the mixture becomes dry and hard, as it will continue cooking in the heat from the pan.

Serves 2

Note: Never overcook scrambled eggs, or try to cook too many eggs at one time.

Scrambled Eggs - Variations

Once you can make scrambled eggs that are light and delicious, then there are a number of variations you can serve to provide a good range of quick and simple snacks on your menu.

To the basic recipe you can add:

3 oz/75 g cooked, diced chicken or rabbit or ham

3 spears chopped, cooked asparagus

2 tablespoons/2 x 15 ml spoons sweetcorn

4 oz/100 g cooked smoked fish, e.g. haddock, kipper

4 oz/100 g mushrooms, sliced thinly and sautéed in butter

2 rashers streaky bacon, chopped and sautéed

2 lambs' kidneys, chopped and lightly sautéed in butter

2-3 tablespoons/2-3 x 15 ml spoons cooked mixed vegetables

Remember to garnish with something colourful, for example parsley sprigs, chopped chervil, celery leaves, sliced or quartered tomatoes.

Fluffy Omelette

4 eggs, separated
¼ teaspoon/¼ x 5 ml spoon salt
pinch cayenne pepper
5 tablespoons/5 x 15 ml spoons water or milk
1 teaspoon/1 x 5 ml spoon baking powder
1 tablespoon/1 x 15 ml spoon melted butter

Place the egg whites in a large bowl, together with salt and pepper, and whisk until dry and firm. Place a plate over the bowl to expel the air.

In another bowl, beat the egg yolks, water or milk and baking powder.

Melt the butter in an omelette pan, over a low heat. Carefully fold the whisked egg whites into the yolk mixture. When the butter is sizzling, pour the omelette mixture into the pan. Cook over a low heat, preferably with a lid on the pan, for 1 minute. Remove the lid and slash the mixture to allow the uncooked egg to run through. (It is far better to cook the omelette slowly and thoroughly than to hurry it.)

To fold the omelette, mark a cut in the place where you want to fold it, spread with filling and turn the pan so that the omelette folds as it slips onto the plate.
Serves 2

Note: It is not a good idea to cook more than 4 eggs at a time for a fluffy omelette, as it will not be cooked evenly.

Omelette aux Fines Herbes

Use the ingredients as for the fluffy omelette recipe, but omit the baking powder and do not separate the eggs. You will also need 1 tablespoon/1 x 15 ml spoon fresh chopped herbs, for example parsley, chervil, chives or tarragon, plus a little crushed garlic.

Beat the eggs, water, salt and pepper together, pour into the pan onto the sizzling butter, and scatter the surface with herbs and garlic.

Do not cover the pan, but cook fairly quickly, allowing the uncooked mixture to run through to the base of the pan.

Omelette – Variations

Any filling to be served inside the omelette should be prepared in advance, ready to add just before folding and serving. Some suggested fillings are:

chopped, sautéed mushrooms
chopped, grilled bacon
flaked, cooked haddock
grated hard cheese
whole fresh, canned or frozen prawns
chopped, sautéed tomatoes with a pinch of basil

For a sweet omelette, follow the recipe for fluffy omelette but add 1 tablespoon of caster sugar to the egg yolks and, when the omelette is cooked, spread it quickly with warmed apricot, strawberry or Morello cherry jam.

Shirred Eggs

2 eggs, separated
salt and pepper

Whip the egg whites in a large bowl, until they are stiff and dry. Divide them between two well-greased ramekin dishes or straight-sided ovenproof dishes.

Make a well in the centre of each, and drop an egg yolk into each cavity. Season with salt and pepper.

Bake in the centre of a moderate oven, mark 4, 350°F/180°C, for 10 minutes.
Serves 1

Note: You may, of course, place the two-egg mixture into one slightly larger dish for easier serving. You will need to serve two shirred eggs per portion, for a very popular snack.

Stuffed Eggs

Take one or two hard-boiled eggs per portion and slice each horizontally.

Remove the yolk mixture from the cavities, and mix with a suitable stuffing, such as a little softened butter and grated cheese, tomato purée, or chopped chicken moistened in a little white sauce. Fill the cavities with this.

Serve hot with a tasty sauce and garnished with some mushrooms or parsley, or cold with a salad.

Pancakes

1½ lb/750 g plain flour
½ teaspoon/½ x 5 ml spoon salt
6-7 eggs
3½ pints/2 litres milk
butter for frying

Sift the flour and salt into a large bowl. Make a well in the centre and drop the eggs into this. Pour in a little of the milk, then beat, either by hand or using an electric mixer, until a thick batter is formed. Add the remaining milk, and allow to stand in a cool place or in the refrigerator for about ½ to 1 hour.

Melt a little butter in the pancake pan and, when it is sizzling, pour a little batter into the pan, enough thinly to coat the base of the pan.

Cook the pancake on one side, then toss or turn over and cook the other side. Roll pancakes up with or without the filling, and serve.

Enough for 40 pancakes, 20 portions

Note: Cooked pancakes may be layered between sheets of greased greaseproof paper and kept hot in a cool oven. Alternatively they may be frozen in this way, and reheated in a hot pan.

Stuffed pancakes never fail to please. Fillings, such as a mushroom filling, may be bound with a little white sauce. For 40 pancakes, mix together in a double saucepan 1½ lb/750 g chopped mushrooms, lightly sautéed, 4 slices of white bread, made into crumbs, and ¾ pint/ 450 ml white sauce. Simply delicious!

Pancakes with Fish Filling

Recipe for pancake batter
1 lb/500 g cooked or canned fish
8 oz/225 g button mushrooms, sliced and sautéed
2 tablespoons/2 x 15 ml spoons parsley, chopped
3 slices white bread, made into crumbs
salt and pepper
1 x 5 oz/150 ml carton soured cream

Make up and fry the pancakes as directed in the previous recipe.

Meanwhile, place the ingredients for the filling in a large basin, mix thoroughly together. Stuff the pancakes with this mixture. Place on a serving dish and heat under a low grill until the filling is hot and the top of the pancakes are crisp.
Serves 20

VEGETARIAN DISHES

It is a sensible idea to offer some vegetarian dishes on your menu.

Crispy Cheese Pie

8 oz/225 g butter or margarine
20 slices brown bread, crusts removed
1 lb/500 g strong cheese, grated
8 eggs, beaten
2¼ pints/1.25 litres milk
2 teaspoons/2 x 5 ml spoons salt
1 tablespoon 1 x 15 ml spoon mustard powder
2 teaspoons/2 x 5 ml spoons paprika

Spread the butter onto the slices of bread, then cut the slices into triangles or cubes. Place a layer of these in the base of a large shallow 4-pint/2.5-litre ovenproof dish or individual dishes, and sprinkle with most of the cheese.

Beat together, in a large bowl, the eggs, milk, salt, mustard and paprika, then pour over the bread. Sprinkle remaining cheese on top.

Bake in the centre of a moderate oven, mark 4, 350°F/180°C for 20-30 minutes. Serve hot.
Serves 16

Noodles with Paprika Sauce

3 lb/1.5 kg noodles
6 tablespoons/6 x 15 ml spoons olive oil
8 oz/225 g plain flour
salt
2 pints/1.2 litres milk
2 tablespoons/2 x 15 ml spoons paprika
grated Parmesan cheese

Cook the noodles in plenty of salted water, until just soft, for about 10-12 minutes. (Never overcook pasta.) Drain thoroughly and keep hot.

Meanwhile, place the remaining ingredients, except the Parmesan cheese, in a large saucepan, and slowly bring to the boil, stirring constantly until the sauce becomes thick. Cook for 1 minute, stirring again.

Serve the noodles on a large flat serving dish, pour the sauce over and serve hot, with grated Parmesan cheese handed separately.
Serves 12

Note: Try to serve pasta in as many ways as possible. Make sure that savoury sauces have plenty of tomato purée and herbs in them - and garlic, too.

Onion Pasties

3 lb/1.5 kg plain flour
1 teaspoon/1 x 5 ml spoon salt
1 lb/500 g margarine and lard mixed
water
4 oz/100 g butter
4 lb/1.75 kg onions, chopped
1 teaspoon/1 x 5 ml spoon garlic salt
1 teaspoon/1 x 5 ml spoon celery salt
pepper

Sift together the flour and salt and add the mixed fats, cut into small pieces. With the tips of the fingers, rub the fat into the flour, until it resembles fine breadcrumbs. Stir in enough cold water to make a firm dough. Roll out the pastry to a thickness of ¼ inch/5 mm.

Meanwhile prepare the filling. Place the butter in a small saucepan and allow it to melt. Add the chopped onions and fry with garlic and celery salts and pepper for 10 minutes.

Cut the pastry into 20 circles about 6 inches/15 cm in diameter. Place a heaped tablespoonful/15 ml spoonful of the filling onto each round. Dampen the rim and gather up the edges to make pasty shapes. Place on a greased baking tray.

Bake in a moderately hot oven, mark 6, 400°F/200°C for 25 minutes.
Serves 20

Potato Cheese Balls

7 lb/3 kg cooked potato, mashed
20 x 1 inch/2.5 cm cubes strong cheese
4 eggs, beaten
2 oz/50 g cornflakes, crushed

Divide the mashed potato into 20 portions, and roll each into a ball with a cube of cheese enclosed inside each.

Coat the balls in beaten egg and then roll each in crushed cornflakes.

Place the potato cheese balls on greased baking trays, and bake in the centre of a moderately hot oven, mark 5, 375°F/190°C, for 25 minutes.

Potato balls make an ideal accompaniment to a less substantial dish, or they may be served on their own with a mixed salad.

Serves 20

Note: This is obviously an excellent way of using up mashed potato.

Potato Boats

20 large potatoes, baked in the oven
½ pint/300 ml cooking oil
¼ pint/150 ml hot milk
salt and cayenne pepper
2 egg whites
3 oz/75 g strong cheese

Cut each baked potato in half lengthwise, and scoop out most of the potato.

Place this mashed potato in a bowl and add the oil, hot milk, salt and pepper.

Whip the egg whites until stiff, then carefully fold them into the potato mixture.

Divide this filling between the potato shells and sprinkle cheese on top.

Place the potato boats on greased baking trays, and bake on the top shelf of a hot oven, mark 8, 450°F/230°C, for 10 minutes or brown under a hot grill. Serve hot.
Serves 20

Tomato Dumplings

20 large tomatoes
4 lb/1.75 kg self-raising flour
salt and pepper
1½ lb/750 g lard
cold water

Peel the tomatoes by placing them in a large bowl of boiling water and then plunging them into cold water to split their skins.

Sift together the flour, salt and pepper into a large bowl. With the tips of the fingers, rub the lard into the flour until it resembles fine breadcrumbs. Add enough cold water to mix to a firm dough.

Roll out the pastry to a thickness of about ¼ inch/5 mm, and cut into circles large enough completely to coat the tomatoes.

Place one tomato on each circle of pastry, brush the rim with a little water and gather up the edges to enclose the tomatoes.

Place on greased baking trays and bake in the centre of a moderately hot oven, mark 6, 400°F/200°C, for about 30 minutes.

Serve piping hot, and, if liked, they may be served with a rich cheese sauce.

Serves 20

Tomato Flan

3 lb/1.5 kg plain flour
salt and pepper
2 lb/1 kg margarine and lard mixed
cold water
6 eggs, beaten
1½ pints/900 ml milk
5 lb/2.25 kg tomatoes, skinned and sliced
6 oz/175 g strong cheese, grated

Sift together the flour, salt and pepper into a large bowl. With the tips of the fingers, rub in the fats until the mixture resembles fine breadcrumbs. Stir in enough cold water to bind to a stiff dough.

Roll out the pastry and use to line 5 x 7-inch/18-cm flan rings, reserving the trimmings.

Arrange the slices of tomato in the flan ring (a little sugar may be added too, if the tomatoes are quite acidic).

Beat together the eggs, milk, salt and pepper and pour this into the prepared flan rings. Sprinkle the grated cheese on top.

Place in a moderately hot oven, mark 6, 400°F/200°C, for 30-45 minutes, or until firm to the touch and golden brown. Serve hot.
Serves 20

Note: If you have any pastry trimmings, they can be re-rolled and cut into strips. These may be placed over each flan, in a lattice design, prior to baking.

Welsh Rarebit

2 oz/50 g butter
½ pint/300 ml beer
1½ lb/750 g Cheddar cheese, grated
3 eggs, beaten
2 teaspoons/2 x 5 ml spoons Worcestershire sauce
2 teaspoons/2 x 5 ml spoons salt
generous pinch of cayenne pepper
12 slices hot buttered toast

Place the butter and beer together in the top of a double boiler, and allow to heat slightly. Stir in the grated cheese. Do not let the mixture become overheated, or it will become stringy.

Add the beaten eggs, Worcestershire sauce, salt and pepper and heat again until well mixed.

Pour the mixture over the slices of hot buttered toast.

Serve immediately.

Serves 12

Note: It is not advisable to make too large a quantity of this mixture at one time.

A poached egg placed on top, just before serving, makes a buck rarebit - a satisfying dish for lunch.

MAIN MEALS

Some of the dishes in this section are less substantial than others and may be served as snacks. A more expensive dish may be followed by a cheaper pudding, or a small supplementary charge could be made, if you have a set, fixed price, menu.

Remember that, if a recipe calls for a certain quantity of, for example, cooked peas, you may substitute, for example, cooked sweetcorn if you have some left over. Use up what is available.

Dried bread may be saved for use in dishes in which breadcrumbs are required; for a stuffing for roast joints of meat and for recipes calling for bread to be soaked, for example barbecued ham loaf or liver dumplings. It may also be used for croûtons for soups (see soup section for ideas) and for puddings requiring breadcrumbs.

If you plan for the following day a recipe using mashed potatoes, cook enough on the previous day to save time and fuel.

Small pieces of meat and vegetables may be used in soups and pies. Pieces of fat should not be wasted, but rendered down in the oven at the end of the day. Do not, however, add any starchy substance to the stock pot; starch turns stock sour very quickly.

Barbecued Ham Loaf

3 lb/1.5 kg white or brown bread, crusts removed
water
1 lb/500 g onions, minced
3 oz/75 g margarine or dripping
4 lb/2 kg ham or bacon, minced
3 lb/1.5 kg liver sausage
6 eggs, beaten
8 oz/225 g semolina
salt and pepper

Barbecue Sauce
¼ pint/150 ml olive oil
1 tablespoon/1 x 15 ml spoon soy sauce
3 cloves garlic, crushed
2 teaspoons/2 x 5 ml spoons salt
4 tablespoons/4 x 15 ml spoons tomato purée
brown sugar

Place the bread in a basin and pour over enough water to moisten it slightly.

Place the onions and margarine or dripping in a pan and fry until softened.

Mix together in a large bowl the minced ham and liver sausage, stir in the softened bread and fried minced onion. Stir in the beaten eggs and semolina, then season with salt and pepper.

Place the mixture in well-greased roly poly tins (sleeves). Bake in the centre of a moderately hot oven, mark 5, 375°F/190°C, for 1 hour or until the loaf is set and golden brown.

Keep the loaves warm whilst preparing the

quantity of sauce you require, and serve hot.

For the barbecue sauce, place all the ingredients in a large saucepan and slowly heat, stirring constantly, until the sauce comes to the boil. Reduce the heat and simmer for a few minutes. Add a little brown sugar if the sauce tastes too acidic.

Slice the ham loaf and pour barbecue sauce over each serving, or hand this separately in a sauce boat.

Serves 28

Note: The ham loaf may be steamed if oven space is limited, and should take about 2½ hours. It is also delicious sliced and served cold with a mixed salad.

Beef Stew

2 lb/1 kg salt pork, chopped
8 lb/3.5 kg stewing steak, chopped
8 tablespoons/8 x 15 ml spoons flour
salt and pepper
5-6 cloves garlic, crushed
6 large onions, chopped
6 beef stock cubes, crumbled
3 pints/1.75 litres water, boiling
tomato ketchup or purée
24 peppercorns, ground
6 cloves
3 bay leaves
3 oz/75 g parsley, chopped
18 large potatoes, sliced thinly
14 large carrots, sliced thinly
2 heads celery, chopped
½ pint/300 ml red wine (optional, but delicious)

Place the pork in a large saucepan and sauté in its own fat. Toss the stewing steak in seasoned flour, stir into the pork and cook over a medium heat for 5-10 minutes until well browned.

Add the crushed garlic, chopped onions, stock cubes, boiling water, tomato ketchup or purée, ground peppercorns, cloves, bay leaves and chopped parsley. Simmer for about 3 hours.

Cook the sliced potatoes, carrots and celery for about 10 minutes, in plenty of boiling, salted water, then drain. Add to the stew for the last 15 minutes of cooking time, together with the wine.
Serves 30

Chicken Pot Pie

3 dressed boiling fowls
good pinch dried rosemary
water
salt
cayenne pepper
2 lb/1 kg self-raising flour
6 eggs, beaten
2½ pints/1.5 litres milk
6 tablespoons/6 x 15 ml spoons melted margarine

Cut the boiling fowl into joints and place them in a large saucepan, together with the rosemary and enough water to cover. Add 2 tablespoons/2 x 15 ml spoons salt and cayenne pepper. Bring to the boil, reduce the heat, and simmer for 1 hour, or until tender. Strain and reserve the stock.

Remove the flesh from the bones, and divide this meat between pie dishes. Pour a little strained stock over each.

Sift together the flour and a pinch of salt into a large bowl. Add the beaten eggs, milk and melted margarine, and beat together thoroughly to form a batter. Pour an equal amount of batter into each pie dish.

Place dishes in the centre of a moderate oven, mark 4, 350°F/180°C, and bake for 30-40 minutes, or until golden brown on top. Add more strained chicken stock to the pies if necessary. Serve hot.

Serves 18

Liver dumplings

18 slices white bread, crusts removed
water
3 lb/1.5 kg cooked lambs' liver, minced
4 lb/1.75 kg liver sausage, diced
6 eggs, separated
2 tablespoons/2 x 15 ml spoons chopped onions
6 oz/175 g dripping, melted
2 tablespoons/2 x 15 ml spoons chopped parsley
salt and pepper
8 oz/225 g flour
5 pints/2.75 litres boiling stock

Place the slices of bread in a large basin, then cover with enough water to moisten. Squeeze the bread to remove excess water, then add the minced liver and cubed liver sausage.

Stir in the egg yolks, onions, dripping, parsley, salt and pepper, and enough flour to bind to make into a stiff consistency.

Form the dough into balls, using floured hands to do so. Make the balls about 1½ inches/3.5 cm in diameter.

Have ready a large pan of the boiling stock (preferably beef stock) and place the liver dumplings in this, one at a time.

Boil the dumplings for about 5 minutes each, never try to cook too many at once.

Serve hot, with freshly cooked rice or pasta and vegetables in season.

Serves 30

Pigs In Blankets

6 oz/175 g onions, minced
2 oz/50 g parsley, chopped finely
7 lb/3 kg cooked potato, mashed
20 thick pork sausages
browned breadcrumbs or crushed cornflakes
2 eggs, beaten
deep fat or oil for frying
apple sauce to serve

In a large bowl, mix together the minced onion and chopped parsley, then beat in the mashed potato and divide this mixture into 20 portions.

Take each sausage and roll it in the portion of potato, then in the breadcrumbs or cornflakes.

Dip each sausage in the beaten egg, then again into the crumbs so that it is thoroughly coated.

Lower the sausages into the hot fat or oil, and deep fry for about 10 minutes, or until the coating is crisp and golden and the sausages are thoroughly cooked inside.

Drain well, then serve hot with apple sauce, and chipped potatoes and peas.
Serves 20

Note: This is a perfect dish to serve on a cold day.

Carbonnade Flamande

3 lb/1.5 kg onions, thinly sliced
12 oz/350 g butter or dripping
7 lb/3 kg stewing steak, diced
3 cloves garlic, crushed
½ teaspoon/½ x 5 ml spoon grated nutmeg
½ teaspoon/½ x 5 ml spoon dried thyme
salt and pepper
3 pints/1.75 litres lager or light ale
3 tablespoons/3 x 15 ml spoons brown sugar
flour

Place the onions and a little of the butter or dripping in a large saucepan, and fry until soft. Drain them and keep hot.

Add the rest of the butter or dripping to the pan and brown the meat in it, on all sides.

Return the onions to the pan together with the crushed garlic, grated nutmeg, thyme, salt and pepper and lager or beer.

Cover the pan, and bring the ingredients to the boil, then reduce the heat and simmer for about 1½ hours, stirring occasionally.

When cooked, if the gravy is too thin, blend a little flour with some cold water to make a 'cream', and use this to thicken the gravy. Bring back to the boil to cook the flour for 5 minutes.

Serve hot with boiled or baked potatoes, and vegetables in season.

Serves 20

Arabian Stewed Lamb with Prunes

5 lb/2.25 kg neck or breast of lamb
2 tablespoons/2 x 15 ml spoons flour
salt and pepper
4 oz/100 g margarine or dripping
5 large onions, chopped
1 teaspoon/1 x 5 ml spoon saffron
1 teaspoon/1 x 5 ml spoon ground cinnamon
hot water
1 lb/500 g soaked prunes
4 teaspoons/4 x 5 ml spoons brown sugar

Cut the meat into chunks about 2 inches x ½ inch/5 cm x 1 cm and coat these in flour, seasoned with salt and pepper. Melt the margarine or dripping in a large saucepan, and add the onions and meat chunks and fry together for about 5 minutes, stirring constantly, until they are brown.

Stir in the saffron, cinnamon and enough hot water to cover the ingredients in the pan. Bring to the boil. Reduce the heat, cover the pan, and simmer for about 2 hours.

Stir in the prunes and sugar, return to the heat and cover again, then simmer for 1 hour.

Serve hot, with vegetables in season.

Serves 12-15

Note: If hotplate space is limited on the cooker, this dish, once the initial frying has been done, may be cooked in a moderate oven, mark 3, 325°F/170°C, for the same length of time.

Goulash Szegedin

1½ lb/750 g fat bacon or pickled pork, diced
5 lb/2.25 kg pork, cubed
15 large onions, sliced
3 tablespoons/3 x 15 ml spoons paprika
water
1 tablespoon/1 x 15 ml spoon sugar
salt and pepper
1 tablespoon/1 x 15 ml spoon caraway seeds
4 cloves garlic, crushed
5 lb/2.25 kg sauerkraut

Place the bacon, pork and onions in a large saucepan, and fry together in the bacon fat until golden brown.

Add the paprika and a little water to cover. Stir in the sugar, salt and pepper, caraway seeds and crushed garlic. Simmer over a gentle heat for about 1½ hours.

Add the sauerkraut and more water if necessary, reheat, then simmer for a further 30 minutes.

Serve very hot, with potatoes baked in their jackets or, alternatively, plain boiled rice or pasta.

Serves 20

Note: This recipe makes a very rich tasting goulash and should be served, traditionally, with jacket potatoes.

SALADS

It is important to get a reputation for preparing good, interesting salads. Never be satisfied with a simple mixture of lettuce, tomato, cucumber and cold meat, tinted with beetroot and beetroot juice!

If possible, try to serve individual salads. The appearance of a large bowl of salad is often spoiled after a few servings, and the best ingredients are usually chosen first.

Tomato Salad

6 lb/2.5 kg ripe tomatoes, sliced thinly
2 bunches spring onions, finely chopped
1 lb/500 g brown sugar
1 pint/600 ml tarragon vinegar
salt and pepper

Arrange the sliced tomatoes in individual dishes or in larger serving dishes. Scatter the chopped spring onions on top, then sprinkle with brown sugar. Allow to stand for about 10 minutes. Pour the vinegar over, then serve immediately.
Serves 20

Note: For the best results, you must use brown sugar and tarragon vinegar, no substitute will do.

Cardinal Salad

2 cans diced beetroot (reserve the juice)
2 packets lemon jelly
1 pint/600 ml boiling water
1 teaspoon/1 x 5 ml spoon salt
4 teaspoons/4 x 5 ml spoon grated horseradish
4 teaspoons/4 x 5 ml spoons grated onion
1 lb/500 g celery, finely diced
3 tablespoons/3 x 15 ml spoons wine vinegar
mixed salad

Drain the beetroot and reserve the juice. Make up the lemon jellies to 1 pint/600 ml with boiling water, then add the beet juice and wine vinegar, to make up to 2 pints/1.2 litres. Add the salt, horseradish and onion.

Allow almost to set, then add the chopped beetroot and celery. Pour this mixture into 20 individual moulds and set them in the refrigerator.

When ready to serve, unmould the cardinal salads and surround each, on an individual plate, with a colourful mixed salad.

Serve chilled.

Serves 20

Cooked Vegetable Salad

1 lb/500 g French beans, sliced and cooked
3 lb/1.5 kg fresh peas, cooked
1 lb/500 g baby carrots, cooked whole
10 green olives, sliced
1 bunch asparagus, cooked
2 lb/1 kg new baby potatoes, cooked (or canned)
1½ pints/900 ml home-made mayonnaise (see page 123)
shredded lettuce or endive

Place all the cooked vegetables together in a large bowl and toss them thoroughly to mix. Coat in mayonnaise and toss well together.

Place a bed of shredded lettuce or endive on a large flat serving platter or on individual plates, then pile the cooked vegetables on top.

Serve with a selection of cold meats or pork slices. Serve cold.
Serves 20

Note: Cook the vegetables separately and take care not to overcook them. For the best results, mix them with the mayonnaise before they are quite cold.

Fish In Aspic

5 lb/2.25 kg raw fish (mixed varieties are best)
5 pints/2.75 litres water
8 sticks celery, roughly chopped
2 small shallots, sliced
6 peppercorns
2 teaspoons/2 x 5 ml spoons dried tarragon
1 teaspoon/1 x 5 ml spoon paprika
2 teaspoons/2 x 5 ml spoons salt
¼ pint/150 ml lemon juice
6 tablespoons/6 x 5 ml spoons powdered gelatine
3 tablespoons/3 x 15 ml spoons capers
1 tablespoon/1 x 15 ml spoon juice from capers
¼ pint/150 ml wine vinegar

Place the fish and water in a large saucepan. Add the celery, shallots, peppercorns, tarragon, paprika, and bring slowly to the boil. Reduce the heat, then simmer with a lid on the pan, for about 10 minutes, or until the fish is tender.

Drain the fish and reserve the fish stock.

Soak the gelatine in a little of the stock, then dissolve it in 3½ pints/2 litres of the hot strained stock. Add the capers and juice, wine vinegar, and salt and pepper if necessary. Chill until it begins to thicken slightly. Arrange layers of the fish and jelly in small individual moulds or larger moulds. Chill until set in the refrigerator.

Turn out on a bed of green salad. Serve chilled.
Serves 20

Note: This dish has a really delicious flavour.

Crunchy Winter Salad

2 cloves garlic, peeled
2 large white Dutch cabbages, finely shredded or chopped
1 lb/500 g Jerusalem artichokes, grated
1 lb/500 g carrots, coarsely grated
2 lb/1 kg red-skinned eating apples, cored and roughly chopped
2 pints/1.2 litres mayonnaise or salad cream

Rub the salad bowls with the cut cloves of garlic. Mix together the prepared vegetables and the apples, and toss them well together in the salad bowls. Coat with mayonnaise or salad cream. Serve chilled.
Serves 24

Salad Dressings

Salad Cream

2 oz/50 g margarine or butter
2 oz/50 g flour
½ oz/15 g cornflour
1 teaspoon/1 x 5 ml spoon mustard powder
2 teaspoons/2 x 5 ml spoons sugar
1 teaspoon/1 x 5 ml spoon salt
1⅛ pints/630 ml warm milk
1 egg, beaten
vinegar

Place the margarine or butter in a large saucepan. Melt over a low heat and stir in the flour, cornflour, mustard, sugar and salt. Cook for 1 minute, stirring constantly.

Remove from the heat and stir in the milk, a little at a time. Return to the heat and bring to the boil, stirring constantly. Boil for 1 minute.

Allow the sauce to cool slightly, then beat in the beaten egg.

Stir in enough vinegar, drop by drop, to give a soft pouring consistency and a satisfactory taste.
Makes 2 pints/1.2 litres

Note: This salad cream stores well for several weeks if kept in jars or lidded containers in the refrigerator.

Mayonnaise

4 egg yolks
2 teaspoons/2 x 5 ml spoons salt
1 teaspoon/1 x 5 ml spoon mustard powder
good pinch cayenne pepper
good pinch sugar
1 pint/600 ml olive oil
4-5 tablespoons/4-5 x 15 ml spoons cider or tarragon vinegar

Place the egg yolks, which should be at room temperature, in a large clean bowl. Add the salt, mustard, cayenne and sugar and beat lightly to mix these together.

Carefully dribble the oil onto the egg yolks, beating constantly, until it has all been incorporated.

To thin down the mixture from time to time, pour in a little of the vinegar, then continue beating in the oil.

Makes 1 pint/600 ml

Note: Mayonnaise may be made in a blender or mixer; check the manufacturer's recommendations in the recipe book provided with the appliance. However it is made, mayonnaise when home-made is delicious and well worth the time spent on making it! It cannot be hurried, since the egg may curdle. If, however, this should happen to you, take another clean bowl, place a fresh egg in it and add the curdled mixture to the fresh egg, beating as before, until the whole of the curdled mix has been added.

French Dressing (Vinaigrette)

2 teaspoons/2 x 5 ml spoons salt
1 teaspoon/1 x 5 ml spoon pepper
½ teaspoon/½ x 5 ml spoon mustard powder
½ teaspoon/½ x 5 ml spoon sugar
¼ pint/150 ml lemon juice or wine or cider vinegar
¾ pint/450 ml olive oil or salad oil

Place all the ingredients in a lidded container or a screw-topped jar. Just before serving, shake vigorously, then use as necessary.
Makes 1 pint/600 ml

Note: Vinaigrette separates out when it stands, so do not dress salads with it until you are ready to serve. It will store for several weeks in a cool place, but do not refrigerate. Shake vigorously as you require it.

SANDWICH IDEAS AND GARNISHES

Sandwiches with plenty of tasty filling can become extremely popular with customers, and are profitable. Remember that many people in colder weather prefer their sandwiches toasted. Open sandwiches can be served with a side-salad to provide a little colour and extra nourishment.

Sandwiches *do not* have to be made with white bread; use brown or wholemeal bread to make a well-balanced snack.

Prepare a variety of fillings that you may need for a lunchtime session, and, if the bread is buttered in readiness too, sandwiches are quick to make up when they are ordered.

Sandwiches will freeze very well, and may be made in large quantities of each flavour, then frozen ready for use when required. Do remember, though, that watery ingredients, for example sliced tomatoes, cucumber, lettuce and celery, do not freeze satisfactorily, but for cheese, meat and paste-type fillings, this may save no end of time.

Try serving bacon sandwiches; other customers will smell the bacon cooking and follow suit!

Decker sandwiches are an interesting variation; for example crisp bacon with lettuce and tomato and cucumber slices.

Always spread butter to the edges of the slice of bread. When using lettuce as part of a sandwich filling, it is a good idea to put the lettuce on the bottom slice and place the filling on top. This way, the sandwich is much easier to cut and to handle.

Easter Sandwich

½ oz/15 g butter
½ green pepper, de-seeded and chopped
1 large egg, beaten
salt and pepper
1 tablespoon/1 x 15 ml spoon milk
3 sardines, drained of oil
2 slices toast
butter for spreading
tomato quarters

Melt the butter in a small saucepan (preferably the non-stick variety). Fry the green pepper until soft, then add the egg, salt, pepper and milk and scramble the egg lightly.

Lay the sardines on one slice of buttered toast. Top with the scrambled egg and pepper, then place the second slice of buttered toast on top.

Cut into fingers and serve hot, garnished with tomato quarters.

Serves 1

Baked Bean Club Sandwich

2 oz/50 g cold canned baked beans
1 rasher grilled bacon
2 tomato slices
2 slices hot buttered toast
1-2 lettuce leaves

Arrange layers of the ingredients on the first slice of buttered toast.

Top with the second slice of toast, and garnish with lettuce and tomato slices.

Serve with mayonnaise if liked.

Serves 1

Peanut Butter Toasty

1 tablespoon/1 x 15 ml spoon chopped ham
1 tablespoon/1 x 15 ml spoon chopped celery
2 tablespoons/2 x 15 ml spoons peanut butter
2 slices wholemeal bread
lettuce leaves

Mix together the ham and celery.

Spread the peanut butter onto the slices of bread. Sprinkle the ham and celery on one slice. Top with the other slice of bread.

Toast under a hot grill, and serve hot, garnished with lettuce leaves.

Serves 1

Hot Chicken à la King Sandwich

4 oz/100 g chicken in white sauce
4 slices toasted wholemeal bread
4 tablespoons/4 x 15 ml spoons cheese sauce
potato crisps

Make up sandwiches using the chicken in white sauce as the filling. Spoon a little of the cheese sauce over each round, then place the sandwiches under a hot grill. Grill until golden and bubbling on top. Serve hot, cut into halves.

Surround the sandwiches with potato crisps.

Serves 2

Roquefort Toast

2 tablespoons/2 x 15 ml spoons chopped watercress
salt
1 tablespoon/1 x 15 ml spoon Roquefort cheese, softened
1 tablespoon/1 x 15 ml spoon mayonnaise
1 hard-boiled egg, sliced
2 slices white toast

First of all season the watercress with a little salt.

Mix together the cheese and mayonnaise and spread this onto one slice of toast. Arrange most of the watercress and egg slices on top, then cover with the second slice of toast.

Top with the remaining watercress and egg slices as a garnish. Serve hot.

Serves 1

Hot Pilchard Sandwich

20 canned pilchards in tomato sauce
40 slices hot buttered toast
8 oz/225 g strong cheese, thinly sliced
sliced tomatoes

Remove the backbone from each pilchard. Mash the flesh and stir in most of the tomato sauce from the cans.

Divide between 20 slices of hot buttered toast. Lay a slice of cheese on each.

Place under a hot grill to melt the cheese and heat the fish filling, then top each with the remaining slices of hot buttered toast.

Cut each sandwich into four and serve hot, garnished with tomato slices.
Serves 20

Note: There are usually about 6 pilchards to a large (1-lb/500-g) can.

Cheese Spread for Toasted Sandwiches

scant 1 pint/600 ml milk
1 teaspoon/1 x 5 ml spoon mustard powder
2 teaspoons/2 x 5 ml spoons salt
2 lb/1 kg strong cheese, grated
To serve - slices of buttered bread and sliced tomatoes

Place all ingredients for the spread in a basin over a pan of gently simmering water (or use a double boiler if available). Cook gently, stirring constantly, for 15 minutes. When the ingredients are well blended and the spread is thick, allow to cool.

This spread will keep for up to 1 week if stored in a lidded container in the refrigerator.

To use, spread the cheese spread onto slices of buttered bread, make into sandwiches in the normal way, then toast on each side until golden and crisp. Cut each round into quarters and garnish with tomato slices.

Note: For a more substantial snack, a poached egg on top of each sandwich round is delicious!

Suggestions for Garnishing Sandwiches and Savoury Dishes

Fresh garnishes are very important to any dish and they often provide an otherwise plain-looking dish or sandwich with a splash of colour. A garnish can also play a more important part in that it may provide a little extra distinctive flavour or moisture to the finished meal.

Vegetable garnishes

Asparagus - cooked tips
Beetroot - sticks, sliced, chopped and hollowed baby beet cups
Cabbage - raw, shredded and chopped
Carrot - raw and chopped, cut into sticks, grated or curled; cooked and cut into shapes using cocktail cutters
Cauliflower - raw or cooked florets
Cucumber - sliced, chopped, sliced and made into horns
Green pepper - chopped, cut into sticks or rings
Herbs - chopped, sprigs and whole pieces
Lettuce - shredded or torn, small leaves, bed of lettuce
Onions - raw and chopped, cut into rings, and spring onions; cooked and made into cups by scooping out centre, and fried onion rings
Radishes - sliced, whole or made into roses
Tomatoes - sliced, quartered, vandyked and chopped

Garnishes from bread

Fried - cubed as croûtons, fried shapes cut with cocktail cutter

Toasted - triangles, half-moon shapes, fingers

Patties - buttered small slices, baked in patty tins, and stuffed with other colourful garnishing ingredients

Miscellaneous

Apples - chopped and tossed in lemon juice, sliced in lemon juice

Cheese - grated finely or coarsely, cubed, sliced

Eggs - hard boiled and sliced, quartered, halved and stuffed

Fish - anchovy fillets, small sardines

Melon - cubed, cut into balls using a melon baller

Pickles - onions if tiny or silverskin, walnuts, gherkins, etc

DESSERTS

It is always advisable to serve a good selection of puddings, pies and light sweets.

Pastry should be made in fairly small quantities and, if possible, by hand. Puff pastry is not often required in a tearoom; excellent frozen puff pastry can be purchased.

To begin with, here are two kinds of pastry often needed for pies and tarts. I find that the recipe for quick pastry never fails.

Quick Pastry

1 lb/500 g lard or white fat
½ pint/300 ml boiling water
1 lb 9 oz/750 g plain flour
2 teaspoons/2 x 5 ml spoons baking powder
1 teaspoon/1 x 5 ml spoon salt

Cut the lard or fat into small chunks, and place these in a large bowl. Pour over this the boiling water and beat until the mixture is soft and creamy.

Sift into the bowl the dry ingredients, adding a little at a time. As the mixture forms a soft ball, stop beating, cover the pastry and chill it in the refrigerator.

Sweet Pastry (for fruit tarts, etc)

2 lb/1 kg plain flour
14 oz/400 g white fat
4 oz/100 g caster sugar
2 eggs, beaten
¼ pint/150 ml milk
2 teaspoons/ 2 x 5 ml spoons salt

Sift the flour into a large bowl, cut the fat into small pieces, and with a mixer, blend together until the mixture resembles fine breadcrumbs. Stir in the sugar, salt, beaten eggs and milk, and mix until a soft dough is formed. *Do not overmix at this stage.*

Chill the pastry in the refrigerator until required, and use for any sweet pies or tarts.

Note: Always chill well before using, and roll out with cold utensils and cold hands, as the richness of the pastry means that the dough will become sticky if handled a lot or if it comes into contact with warm implements.

Coffee Tarts

20 baked pastry cases
1 pint/600 ml evaporated milk
8 oz/225 g plain flour
8 oz/225 g caster sugar
1 teaspoon/1 x 5 ml spoon salt
½ pint/300 ml strong black coffee
3 eggs, beaten
8 oz/225 g margarine, melted
1 teaspoon/1 x 5 ml spoon vanilla essence
1 pint/600 ml whipping cream, whipped

Make up either the quick pastry or sweet pastry and roll out, cut into 20 circles and fill small tartlet cases with the circles. Prick the bases and bake them blind in the centre of a moderately hot oven, mark 6, 400°F/200°C, for about 7-10 minutes. Cool.

Place the milk and flour in a large saucepan and add the sugar and salt, then stir in the coffee. Cook, stirring constantly, until the mixture thickens.

Stir in the beaten eggs and return to the heat and cook for a further 2 minutes, without boiling. Remove from the heat, add the melted margarine and vanilla essence, and allow to cool slightly.

Fill the tartlet cases with this mixture, and allow to cool completely, then top each with a whirl of whipped cream.

Serves 20

Strawberry Meringue Tarts

1 lb/500 g plain flour
good pinch of salt
12 oz/350 g margarine and lard mixed
cold water
2 lb/1 kg strawberry jam
4 egg whites
6-8 oz/175-225 g caster sugar

Sift together the flour and salt into a large bowl. Rub in the mixed fats with the tips of the fingers. Stir in enough cold water to bind to a stiff dough. Roll out the pastry and use to line 30 small saucers or shallow ovenproof dishes.

Place a large tablespoonful/15 ml spoonful strawberry jam into each pastry case.

Place the saucers on a baking tray and bake in a moderately hot oven, mark 6, 400°F/200°C, for about 15-20 minutes, or until lightly golden.

Whisk the egg whites until stiff, and carefully fold in the sugar. Divide this meringue between the pastry jam tarts, or, if preferred, pipe a whirl of meringue on top of each.

Return the tarts to the oven, reduced in heat to mark 1, 275°F/140°C, for about 20 minutes, to set the meringue. Serve hot or cold, and with whipped cream if liked.
Serves 30

Note: Alter the flavour of the jam used, for example apricot, blackcurrant, lemon curd, and you have an endless variety of flavoured tarts.

Brown Betty

12 oz/350 g soft brown or white breadcrumbs
12 oz/350 g margarine or butter, melted
3 lb/1.5 kg cooking apples, peeled, cored and sliced
12 oz/350 g brown sugar
1 teaspoon 1 x 5 ml spoon ground cinnamon
1 teaspoon/1 x 5 ml spoon grated nutmeg
pinch of salt
grated rind and juice of 2 large lemons
4 tablespoons/4 x 15 ml spoons water

Place the breadcrumbs in a large bowl and stir in the melted butter. Use half of this mixture to line the base of ovenproof dishes.

Arrange the slices of apple on top.

Mix together the brown sugar, cinnamon, nutmeg, salt and grated lemon rind and sprinkle this mixture over the apples.

Mix together the lemon juice and water and sprinkle over the top.

Bake in the centre of a moderate oven, mark 4, 350°F/180°C, for 40-45 minutes, until set and golden brown.

Serve hot or cold, with whipped cream if liked, or with custard.
Serves 16

Note: This is an excellent alternative to the traditional tearoom apple crumble.

Gâteau Isabella

2 lb/1 kg self-raising flour
1 lb/500 g margarine
pinch of salt
1 lb/500 g caster sugar
8 oz/225 g cocoa powder
1 teaspoon/1 x 5 ml spoon vanilla essence
milk to mix
Isabella sauce (page 148)

Sift the flour into a large bowl, add the salt and rub in the margarine, using the tips of the fingers.

Stir in the caster sugar and cocoa powder, and then add the vanilla essence and enough milk to mix to a soft consistency.

Spoon into two greased slab cake tins and place these in the centre of a moderately hot oven, mark 5, 375°F/190°C, for 30 minutes.

Meanwhile prepare the Isabella sauce and, when the chocolate sponge is baked, cut it into portions.

Serve hot, with Isabella sauce poured over each individual portion or served separately, in a sauce boat.

Serves 20

Note: This pudding can taste even better if cooked the day before it is needed. When cold, cut into portions, and warm them through when they are required. It is especially good served cold with a hot sauce.

Ginger Pudding with Apple Sauce

1½ lb/750 g self-raising flour
pinch of salt
1 lb/500 g margarine
1 lb/500 g soft brown sugar
2 teaspoons/2 x 5 ml spoons mixed spice
2 teaspoons/2 x 5 ml spoons ground ginger
1 tablespoon/1 x 15 ml spoon black treacle
warm water to mix
hot apple sauce to serve

Sift together the flour and salt and, with the tips of the fingers, rub in the margarine, until the mixture resembles fine breadcrumbs.

Stir in the sugar, mixed spice, ground ginger and mix well together. Stir in the black treacle and enough warm water to bind to make a firm batter.

Place this batter in two greased and floured slab cake tins.

Place the tins in the centre of a moderately hot oven, mark 5, 375°F/190°C, for 45 minutes or until the pudding is well risen and firm to the touch.

Serve hot, cut into squares, with hot apple sauce.

Serves 15

Note: A good tip is to warm the treacle a little. This makes it easier to use.

Fresh Fruit Whip

6 pints/3.5 litres water
1½ lb/750 g semolina
1½ lb/750 g granulated sugar
1½ lb/750 g freshly stewed fruit and juice
food colouring if necessary
freshly whipped whipping cream

Blend together a little of the water and the semolina, to make a soft 'cream'. Boil the remaining water, then pour this onto the semolina, and return the mixture to the pan with the sugar. Cook over a high heat until it becomes thick, stirring all the time.

Add the fruit and fruit juice, and blend until well mixed.

Allow to become quite cold, then whip this mixture until it is fairly stiff and frothy.

Add colouring, if necessary, to correspond to the flavour of fruit used, then pour into stemmed glasses.

Serve chilled, with freshly whipped cream.
Serves 20

Note: This is a particularly delicious pudding in which to use plums when they are cheap and plentiful. If red plums are used, they give an exotic purple colour to the fruit whip. Alternatively apples, pears, rhubarb, gooseberries, blackberry and apple or blackcurrants may also be used, or a mixture of fresh fruits in season.

Old-Fashioned Queen of Puddings

4 pints/2.25 litres milk
1½ lb/750 g caster sugar
pinch of salt
8 eggs, separated
2 lb/1 kg white bread or cake crumbs
grated rind of 2 lemons
8 oz/225 g butter, melted
1 lb/500 g strawberry jam

Heat the milk and add to this half of the sugar and the salt. Separate the eggs, and pour the yolks into the milk and sugar mixture, beat well.

Place the bread or cake crumbs in a large bowl, pour over the milk and egg mixture, and add the lemon rind and melted butter. Mix thoroughly.

Turn this mixture into well-greased baking dishes. Stand these dishes in large tins half filled with water, then bake in a moderate oven, mark 3, 325°F/170°C, for about 30 minutes, or until the pudding is firm on top.

Remove from the oven, spread each pudding with jam.

Whip the egg whites until stiff, stir in the remaining sugar lightly, then place this meringue on top of each pudding, forking up the surface if desired, to form 'peaks'.

Return to the oven, mark 2, 300°F/150°C, for a further 15 minutes, or until the meringue is set and a pale straw colour. Serve hot.

Serves 20

Lemon Freeze

2 oz/50 g cornflakes, crushed
4 tablespoons/4 x 15 ml spoons brown sugar
4 oz/100 g margarine, melted
4 eggs, separated
2 large cans condensed milk
10 tablespoons/10 x 15 ml spoons lemon juice
1 teaspoon/1 x 5 ml spoon grated lemon rind
6 tablespoons/6 x 15 ml spoons sugar

Mix together in a basin the crushed cornflakes, brown sugar and melted margarine, then press this mixture into 2 x 18-inch/45-cm square shallow tins, reserving a few crumbs for the top. Allow these bases to set slightly.

Meanwhile, beat the egg yolks until they are thick and pale, and beat in the condensed milk, lemon juice, grated rind and sugar.

Whip the egg whites until they are stiff, then fold them into the lemon mixture. Turn this into the prepared tins, and smooth the surface level. Scatter the remaining crumbs on top.

Place the tins in a refrigerator to chill and set thoroughly, then cut into fingers or squares and serve chilled.
Serves 15

Note: Lemon freeze makes a splendid pudding on a hot summer's day.

SAUCES

Try to remember that a sauce plays a very important part in cooking and so care must always be taken in the preparation, cooking and serving of sauces, since a poor one can ruin an otherwise delicious meal.

As a rule, 4½ pints/2.5 litres of sauce will be sufficient for 20 helpings. For small quantities use a wooden spoon; for larger, a whisk.

Basic White Pouring Sauce

4 oz/100 g margarine or butter
4 oz/100 g flour
salt and white pepper
4 pints/2.25 litres milk

Melt the butter or margarine in a large saucepan, stir in the flour, salt and pepper, and cook, stirring constantly, over a moderate heat, until the *roux* begins to become granular.

Remove from the heat and stir in the milk, a little at a time. Return to the heat, and bring slowly to the boil, stirring constantly. Cook for a further 3 minutes to ensure that there is no taste of flour, then use as required.

Enough for 20 portions, to pour over cooked foods

Basic Coating Sauce

8 oz/225 g margarine or butter
8 oz/225 g flour
salt and white pepper
4 pints/2.25 litres milk

Proceed as in previous method.

Enough for 20 portions, to coat cooked meat and fish, etc.

Basic Binding Sauce

1 lb/500 g margarine or butter
1 lb/500 g flour
salt and pepper
4 pints/2.25 litres milk

Proceed as for the basic white pouring sauce.

Enough for 20 portions, to bind together ingredients for the base of a soufflé, or in meat or fish pies, or croquettes

Basic White Sauces - Variations

After thickening the sauce stir in any of the following ingredients to taste:

chopped parsley; chopped basil; chopped tarragon; chopped chervil; chopped thyme; chopped shallots; chopped onions; grated nutmeg - a good pinch; 4-6 cloves; 2-4 bay leaves; a good pinch of paprika; a good pinch of curry powder; a pinch of chilli powder; 1 lb/500 g grated cheese; 1 lb/500 g chopped and sautéed mushrooms; tomato purée; crushed garlic; grated rind and juice of 2 lemons; sherry or Madeira to taste; caster sugar to make a sweet white sauce.

All-in-one Method

The all-in-one method is also satisfactory for making the larger amounts of sauce necessary for commercial catering. For this method the amounts of ingredients remain the same, but all the ingredients are placed in the saucepan at once, then stirred together over a moderate heat, until the sauce comes to the boil. At this stage, whisk the sauce vigorously, then cook for a further minute, until the sauce tastes cooked and is ready to serve. Some people prefer to make sauces like this rather than by the *roux* method.

Brown Sauce

8 oz/225 g butter or dripping
4 oz/100 g button mushrooms, chopped
4 onions, quartered
4 carrots, cut into chunks
8 oz/225 g flour
4 pints/2.25 litres brown stock
juice of 1 lemon
salt and black pepper

Place the butter or dripping in a large saucepan, melt slowly, then fry the mushrooms, onions and carrots until they are well browned, but do not let them burn.

Stir in the flour, and cook until it is dark but not burnt.

Remove from the heat, gradually stir in the stock, a little at a time, then return the saucepan to the heat. Bring to the boil, stirring constantly, then add the lemon juice, salt and black pepper.

Reduce the heat and simmer for about 30 minutes, or longer if there is time, so that the sauce becomes a dark brown colour with lots of flavour.

Strain the sauce through a sieve before use.

Enough for 20 portions

Note: Never add gravy browning to a white sauce and serve it as brown sauce.

Sweet Sauces

Apricot Sauce

1 lb/500 g apricot jam
4 pints/2.25 litres water
8 oz/225 g flour
8 oz/225 g caster sugar
4 oz/100 g butter

Heat together the jam and most of the water.

Add the flour, mixed with the remaining water, the sugar and butter, then whisk vigorously over a moderate heat until the sauce is thick and clear.

Use this to cover flans, or to pour over steamed puddings.

Enough for 20 portions

Chocolate Sauce

4½ pints/2.5 litres water
12 oz/350 g flour
8 oz/225 g cocoa powder
1 lb/500 g granulated sugar
2 teaspoons/2 x 5 ml spoons vanilla essence
1 teaspoon/1 x 5 ml spoon salt

Place all ingredients together in a large saucepan, then whisk vigorously until a thick sauce is formed. Simmer to make it thicker if desired. Serve hot or cold.

Enough for 20 portions

Isabella Sauce

4½ pints/2.5 litres strong black coffee
10 oz/275 g flour
8 oz/225 g granulated sugar
1 pint/600 ml lemon squash, undiluted
1 lb/500 g golden syrup

Place all ingredients in a large saucepan, and whisk vigorously, until the sauce becomes thick and syrupy.

Use hot.

Enough for 20 portions

Note: Isabella sauce is quite delicious – it tastes like liquid toffee!

CAKES, CAKE ICINGS AND FILLINGS

Cake-making

The reputation of a tearoom can depend largely upon the quality of cakes, scones and biscuits which are served, so it is time well spent to put together a selection of reliable and interesting recipes, which you know will work.

Cakes, like so many baked goods, are only as good as the ingredients used in them, so remember to choose the right ingredients for the cakes you make.

Sugar – caster sugar must always be used for light sponge and sandwich cakes, whereas granulated may be used for light fruit cakes and rock cakes. Brown sugar (not demerara) is best for rich fruit cakes, gingerbread and tealoaves.

Fats – butter, although it gives a far better flavour to cakes, is not necessarily suitable for all types. It is ideal for rich fruit cakes, where they are to be kept for some time, and for Madeira cakes, etc, but for light sponge and sandwich cakes, butter can give too heavy a texture, so margarine is best. If margarine is to be used, do buy the softer types of table or cooking margarine, and not a hard pastry margarine.

Flour - use a fine grade of flour, and a soft flour at that, for cakes; remember that strong flour is for yeast foods. You will probably have recipes using both self-raising and plain flour, so stick to whichever is required in a particular recipe.

Eggs - keep eggs for cake-making at room temperature, because if they are too cold, they will cause a delicate mixture to curdle. Cracked eggs may be used for cakes, but check that each is fresh before adding it to a mixture. never store eggs, particularly cracked ones for cake-making, near to strong smelling foods, or the flavours will penetrate the shells. An excellent fatless sponge may be made from dried eggs.

Sandwich or Yellow Layer Cake

1 lb/500 g margarine
2 lb/1 kg caster sugar
9 eggs, separated
2½ lb/1.25 kg flour
3 teaspoons/3 x 5 ml spoons baking powder
1 teaspoon/1 x 5 ml spoon salt
2½ pints/1.5 litres milk
2 teaspoons/2 x 5 ml spoons vanilla essence

Make sure that the margarine, sugar, eggs and milk are all at room temperature.

Place the margarine in the bowl of a mixer and cream until it is pale in colour and light in texture. Stir in the sugar, vanilla essence then egg yolks, one at a time, until they are thoroughly blended.

Sift together the flour, salt and baking powder, then add gradually to the creamed mixture. Stir in the milk, as necessary, to make the mixture a manageable consistency.

Whip the egg whites until stiff, then carefully fold them into the mixture.

Divide the mixture between prepared tins, which should be greased and floured, or lined with greased greaseproof paper, beforehand.

Bake 1-lb/500-g loaf cakes at mark 5, 375°F/190°C, for ¾-1 hour; for sandwich cakes, bake at the same temperature, but for 25-30 minutes.

Cool and decorate the cakes with buttercream and glacé icing.

Makes 10 x 1-lb/500-g layers

Sandwich Cake – Variations

Chocolate Cake - Substitute 8 oz/225 g of the flour with 1 lb/500 g cocoa powder and add 4 oz/100 g more margarine.

Seed Cake - Add 2 tablespoons/2 x 15 ml spoons caraway seeds and 2 tablespoons/2 x 15 ml spoons grated lemon rind with the flour and bake the mixture in loaf tins.

Light Fruit Cake - Add 4 lb/1.75 kg mixed dried fruit and 6 oz/175 g mixed peel to the basic mixture after the flour has been added.

Cherry Cake - Add 2 lb/1 kg halved and floured glacé cherries instead of the fruit and peel in the above variation, and 1 teaspoon/1 x 5 ml spoon almond essence instead of the vanilla essence.

Chocolate Chip Cake - Add 2½ lb/1.25 kg chocolate chips or finely chopped couverture to the basic mix. Bake half of the quantity in sandwich tins.

Coffee Cakes - Add 2 tablespoons/2 x 15 ml spoons coffee essence or concentrated powder to the basic mixture. Add to the eggs if using liquid coffee. Mix the coffee with a little hot water or with the flour if you are adding it as a powder.

Marble Cake - Divide the mixture into three, leave one-third plain, add 1 tablespoon/1 x 15 ml spoon chocolate syrup to one-third of the mix and some pink food colouring to the last third. Place spoonfuls of the various mixtures into the tins in alternate colours. Smooth level.

Coconut Layer Cake - Make the basic cakes in sandwich tins (7-inch/18-cm). When cooked and cooled, sandwich together with lightly whipped cream or with marshmallow filling (page 166), then spread white butter icing (page 162) over the tops. Sprinkle each top with shredded coconut before the icing has set. If preferred, pale pink or pale green icing may be used; add the required food colouring to white butter icing.

Walnut Cake - Add 2 lb/1 kg ground or broken walnuts to the basic mixture together with 2 teaspoons/2 x 5 ml spoons grated nutmeg, when the flour is added. Bake in sandwich tins.

Dark Fruit Cake - Make up the basic mixture using soft brown sugar instead of caster, and using the same quantities of fruit as for the light fruit cake. This is a popular variation.

To decorate: use sea foam icing (page 171) or bisque icing (page 170) using a tinted cake mixture. Ice some with butterscotch icing (page 169) or with chocolate fudge icing (page 165) or with plain white icing. Decorate with halved glacé cherries, crystallised violets, silver and mimosa balls, walnut halves or angelica 'leaves' etc.

Or you might choose to flavour a basic glacé icing with orange juice, lemon juice, tangerine or coffee, and colour the icing accordingly.

Dark Chocolate Cake

8 oz/225 g chocolate couverture
1 pint/600 ml boiling water
12 oz/350 g margarine
8 oz/225 g caster sugar
1 teaspoon/1 x 5 ml spoon salt
9 eggs
2 teaspoons/2 x 5 ml spoons vanilla essence
1 pint/600 ml buttermilk
1¾ lb/800 g plain flour
2 teaspoons/2 x 5 ml spoons bicarbonate of soda
3 teaspoons/3 x 5 ml spoons baking powder

Melt the chocolate carefully over a pan of gently simmering water. When the chocolate has melted, stir in the boiling water - but only when it has *completely* melted. Stir until smooth, then allow to cool.

Cream together, in a large bowl, the margarine and sugar until light and fluffy in texture. Add the salt, then the eggs, one at a time, and beat well between each addition.

Add the vanilla essence to the buttermilk.

Sift together the flour, bicarbonate of soda and baking powder, then fold it into the creamed mixture, alternately with the buttermilk.

Grease the bases of cake tins, and divide the mixture between them.

Bake in the centre of a moderate oven, mark 3, 325°F/170°C, for 45 minutes. Cool and cut into squares or slices.

White Cake

1¼ lb/600 g margarine
2¾ lb/1.3 kg caster sugar
9 egg whites
2 teaspoons/2 x 5 ml spoons vanilla or lemon essence
2 pints/1.2 litres water
3 lb 2 oz/1.5 kg plain white flour
4 tablespoons/4 x 15 ml spoons baking powder
freshly whipped double cream to decorate

Soften the margarine slightly in a large bowl or by using an electric mixer, then add the sugar and cream together until light and fluffy.

Beat in the egg whites, then stir in the vanilla or lemon essence and water and beat well.

Sift together the flour and baking powder, and fold into the mixture lightly but thoroughly.

Divide between 1-lb/500-g loaf tins, lined with greaseproof paper, and bake in a moderate oven, mark 4, 350°F/180°C, for 25 minutes, or until firm to the touch.

Either cut the cakes through the centre and sandwich the halves together with whipped cream; or completely cover the surface of the cakes with whipped cream.

Note: This is an exotic cake or gâteau and is particularly popular during the summer as it is so light in texture.

The egg yolks left over may be used to make mayonnaise or added to scrambled eggs, etc.

Apple Sauce Cake

12 oz/350 g butter or margarine
1½ lb/750 g sugar
3 eggs
1 lb 2 oz/550 g plain flour
1 lb/500 g raisins or sultanas
12 oz/350 g currants
4 oz/100 g chopped walnuts
1½ pints/900 ml hot apple sauce
1 teaspoon/1 x 5 ml spoon salt
3 teaspoons/3 x 5 ml spoons bicarbonate of soda
3 teaspoons/3 x 5 ml spoons cinnamon
½ teaspoon/½ x 5 ml spoon ground cloves or nutmeg

Soften the margarine or butter slightly, then add the sugar and cream together until light and fluffy. Stir in the beaten eggs and beat thoroughly.

Sift a little of the flour over the dried fruit and nuts and then sift the rest of the flour together with the hot apple sauce, salt, bicarbonate of soda and the spices. Mix into the egg, sugar and fat mixture, beating thoroughly.

Bake in shallow (3-inch/7.5-cm deep) greased and lined cake tins at mark 3, 325°F/170°C for about 50 minutes, or until firm to the touch.

The cake can be iced with plain water icing and cut into fingers. One glacé cherry or half a walnut on each slice adds interest.

Soft Gingerbread

6 oz/175 g margarine
1 pint/600 ml black treacle
3 teaspoons/3 x 5 ml spoons bicarbonate of soda
1 teaspoon/1 x 5 ml spoon salt
4 teaspoons/4 x 5 ml spoons ground ginger
1 lb/500 g plain flour
½ pint/300 ml yogurt or buttermilk
2 eggs, beaten

Place the margarine and treacle in a large heavy-based saucepan, melt the ingredients and remove from the heat.

Stir in the bicarbonate of soda, salt, ground ginger, then the sifted flour, buttermilk or yogurt and beaten eggs. Mix quickly but thoroughly together, then pour into greased sandwich tins, patty tins or into paper cases.

Bake in a moderate oven, mark 4, 350°F/180°C, for about 20 minutes.

Cup Cakes

2¼ lb/1.1 kg self-raising flour
3 teaspoons/3 x 5 ml spoons baking powder
1 teaspoon/1 x 5 ml spoon salt
1½ lb/750 g soft margarine
2 lb/1 kg caster sugar
4 eggs, beaten
1½ pints/900 ml milk

Sift together the flour, baking powder and salt. Soften the margarine and beat in the sugar and eggs, and mix thoroughly together. Beat for about 3 minutes, then stir in the flour, baking powder and salt. Finally stir in the milk.

Half-fill paper bun cases with the mixture, place these on a baking tray and bake in a moderately hot oven, mark 6, 400°F/200°C, for about 10 minutes, or until well risen and golden on top.

Makes 50-60

Note: This mixture may be coloured pink with food colouring and the cakes iced and decorated.

Rock Cakes

6 oz/175 g margarine
3 oz/75 g soft brown sugar
1 egg, beaten
4 oz/100 g currants or sultanas
12 oz/350 g plain flour
1 tablespoon/1 x 15 ml spoon baking powder

Cream together the margarine and soft brown sugar, until light and fluffy. Stir in the beaten egg and fruit. Sift together the flour and baking powder, then fold into the mixture.

Bind together with the finger tips, then place mounds of this mixture on well-greased baking trays.

Bake in a moderately hot oven, mark 6, 400°F/200°C, for about 10-15 minutes.

Note: Rock cakes are always popular. Try serving them with morning coffee, too.

Quick Cake Ideas:

Devil's Food Cake - Make a dark chocolate cake and fill the centre with white butter cream and ice the top with white glacé icing.

Fudge Cake - Dark chocolate cake with a melted chocolate icing over the top.

Pineapple Cake - Yellow layer or sandwich cake, sandwiched together with cooked pineapple filling (page 172), containing chopped pieces of glacé pineapple. Cover the cake with seven-minute icing (page 168) or whipped cream and scatter more chopped glacé pineapple on top.

Orange Date Cake - Sandwich sponge cakes together with cooked orange filling (page 172) or orange marmalade, and scatter chopped dates in the filling before sandwiching the cake together. Top with orange icing or sifted icing sugar.

Coffee Cake - Make a basic coffee cake and top with coffee icing or coffee butter icing (page 162).

Any of the cakes may be baked in shallow tins and, once cooked, cut into fingers or shapes using pastry cutters. These can be butter iced or dipped into melted fondant or chocolate, and decorated with piped butter icing or with sugared flowers, etc. They may be served in individual paper cases.

Some Common Faults:

Coarse texture to the cake - caused by insufficient flour, oven too cool, mixture not mixed thoroughly enough or fat and sugar creamed too fast in an electric mixer.

Heavy texture to the cake - caused by too much fat or too much sugar, not enough raising agent or oven too cool.

Cracked top to cakes - caused by too much flour, oven too hot, or mixed too heavily and for too long.

Too soft to handle - too much sugar used in the recipe or too much fat or baking powder. Insufficient egg in the mixture or insufficient mixing will also cause this.

Large holes in the texture - not mixed enough, placed in baking tin in a hurry and not smoothed level before baking. Tap the tins on the table before baking to prevent this.

Brown specks on the surface - or a sticky surface - may be caused by the fat and sugar not being creamed together sufficiently.

Uncooked Icings

Butter Icing

8 oz/225 g butter or margarine
1½ lb/750 g sieved icing sugar
flavouring and colouring to taste

Soften the margarine well before you begin, then gradually beat in the sieved icing sugar, until a soft butter icing is formed.

Flavour and colour as necessary; coffee essence is particularly pleasant.

Enough to cover 2 x 1-lb/500-g round cakes

Note: Use to sandwich cakes together and biscuits together and for decorating the tops of cakes. It may be piped onto cakes for a more professional decoration. Butter icing will keep in the refrigerator for several weeks provided that it has been covered and is allowed, when required, to come back to room temperature.

Royal Icing

1 egg white
10 oz/275 g sieved icing sugar
2 teaspoons/2 x 5 ml spoons lemon juice, strained a few drops glycerine if the cake is to be kept for some time.

Beat the egg white slightly, then gradually beat in the sieved icing sugar, until it has all been incorporated. Stir in the lemon juice (to keep the icing really white) and glycerine if the cake is to be kept before being used.

Colour as necessary, but this icing cannot be successfully flavoured.

Enough to cover 1 x 8-inch/20-cm fruit cake

Note: For basic icing on wedding, christening, birthday and Christmas cakes, etc, it is best to use this icing fairly stiff, and smooth it onto a cake already prepared with almond paste.

Royal icing can be thickened with more icing sugar and coloured as necessary in order to be piped on the cake as a decoration.

Fondant Icing

1 lb/500 g sieved icing sugar
1 egg white
1 tablespoon/1 x 15 ml spoon glycerine

Sift the sugar into a large bowl, stir in the egg white and glycerine and work together until the mixture is well blended. Knead the icing well, then roll it out between two sheets of waxed paper, dusted with icing sugar.

To use, the cake should first be prepared with almond paste. Brush the top and sides of the cake with a little honey. Cut out the shape of the top of the cake in icing and place it in position. Smooth with a dry spatula. Repeat with the sides of the cake. Roll out the trimmings or mould them to make flowers which may be tinted pink or yellow.

This is a softer icing than royal icing and easier to apply.

Note: Fondant icing may be bought from a wholesaler, in cans and already coloured, so it is ready for immediate use. Heat it over a pan of simmering water, and use in a semi-liquid state.

Fudge Icing

Use a white glacé icing, sieved icing sugar mixed with warm water to the required consistency, to which you can add a little cocoa powder and a few drops vanilla essence.

Banana Cream Filling

2-3 bananas
1 teaspoon/1 x 5 ml spoon grated lemon rind
2 oz/50 g caster sugar
2 tablespoons/2 x 15 ml spoons double cream

Mash the bananas until soft. Stir in the grated lemon rind and caster sugar and then fold in the cream gently, making sure that the ingredients are thoroughly mixed.

Use immediately, to sandwich cakes together and to decorate the tops of cakes.

This is a cream filling which should be eaten on the day it is made, since it is perishable.

Marshmallow Cream

1 egg white
8 oz/225 g seedless raspberry jam

Place both ingredients in the bowl of an electric mixer and beat for about 10-15 minutes, until thick. Use as required, for sandwiching cakes and biscuits together.

This will keep, if stored covered in the refrigerator, for several days.

Cooked Icings

Basic Boiled Icing

3 lb/1.5 kg granulated sugar
1¾ pints/1 litre water
12 oz/350 g golden syrup
6 egg whites
½ teaspoon/½ x 5 ml spoon salt
3 oz/75 g sieved icing sugar
1 teaspoon/1 x 5 ml spoon vanilla essence

Place the granulated sugar, water and golden syrup in a heavy-based pan. Stir and heat gently until all ingredients are thoroughly dissolved. *Do not allow to boil before the sugar has dissolved.*

Increase the heat and boil until the temperature reaches 232°F/111°C on your sugar thermometer. Remove at once from the heat.

Whip the egg whites and salt together until stiff, then stir in the icing sugar and pour this mixture into the hot syrup, together with the vanilla essence. Continue to beat vigorously, using an electric mixer if possible, until the icing stays in peaks. Use immediately as a frosting for chocolate, walnut and other large cakes.

Enough to cover 9 x 7-inch/18-cm cakes

Baltimore Icing

Boiled icing, as in previous recipe
8 oz/225 g sultanas
8 oz/225 g walnuts, chopped
8 oz/225 g citron peel, chopped
8 oz/225 g glacé cherries, chopped

Mix all the ingredients together and use immediately to cover a plain cake or Madeira cake.

Seven Minute Icing

4 oz/100 g unbeaten egg white
1¼ lb/600 g granulated sugar
5 teaspoons/5 x 5 ml spoons cold water
2 teaspoons/2 x 5 ml spoons liquid glucose

Place the egg whites, granulated sugar and water in the top of a double boiler, or in a bowl over a pan of gently simmering water. Stir to mix thoroughly, then stir in the glucose. Increase the heat so that the water below the icing boils and whisk, preferably with an electric mixer, for 7 minutes exactly. The icing should then stand in peaks.

Spread onto the cakes at once. If colouring is necessary, add it at the very beginning, since time must not be lost once the icing is made.
Enough to cover 4 cakes

Butterscotch Icing

2 lb/1 kg light brown sugar (never use demerara sugar)
3 oz/75 g plain flour
1 pint/600 ml liquid glucose
3 oz/75 g raw egg yolks
12 fl oz/375 ml milk
1 tablespoon/1 x 15 ml spoon lemon juice
2 teaspoons/2 x 5 ml spoons vanilla essence
1 teaspoon/1 x 5 ml spoon salt
1½ oz/40 g butter
½ pint/300 ml cream
2½ lb/1.25 kg icing sugar

Mix the brown sugar and flour together and then beat in the glucose.

Beat the egg yolks, add the milk, and mix into the sugar and flour.

Put the mixture into a pan and boil it to 232°F/111°C.

Take the pan off the heat and add the lemon juice, vanilla essence, salt and butter. Leave to cool slightly and then add the cream and icing sugar.

Ices about 4½ lb/2.25 kg of cake

Bisque Icing

3 lb/1.5 kg granulated sugar
1½ pints/900 ml water
½ pint/300 ml liquid glucose
8 oz/225 g raw egg whites
½ teaspoon/½ x 5 ml spoon salt
3 oz/75 g icing sugar
10 oz/275 g almond macaroons, chopped
1 teaspoon/1 x 5 ml spoon rum flavouring

Put the granulated sugar, water and glucose into a saucepan. Stir until the sugar has dissolved, watching for any crystals and wiping down the sides of the pan with a fork wrapped in damp cotton. Boil the mixture to 232°F/111°C and then remove the pan from the heat.

Put the egg whites and salt into a cold, dry mixing bowl, and, adding the icing sugar slowly, beat at a high speed with an electric whisk for about 2 minutes until the mixture is frothy. Then, while continuing to beat, add the syrup slowly, letting it flow down the sides of the pan. Add the macaroon crumbs and the rum flavouring slowly and lower the beating rate.

When the icing stands in peaks, it is ready. A further test is to dip a knife in the icing and then tap it sharply on the side of the bowl - if the icing comes off, leaving the blade clean, it is ready for use. If it is too hard, add a few drops of hot water. Use at once.

Ices about 4½ lb/2.25 kg of cake

Sea Foam Icing

3 lb/1.5 kg light, soft brown sugar
14 fl oz/420 ml strong coffee
2½ tablespoons/2½ x 15 ml spoons liquid glucose
6 oz/175 g raw egg whites
½ teaspoon/½ x 5 ml spoon salt
5 oz/150 g icing sugar, sifted
a few drops of flavouring

Mix the brown sugar, coffee and glucose in a saucepan and stir, over heat, until the glucose has dissolved. Keep wiping down the sides of the pan with a fork wrapped in damp cotton. Boil to 232°F/111°C without stirring and then remove the pan from the heat.

Put the egg whites and salt in a cold, dry mixing bowl. Slowly add the icing sugar while beating the mixture continuously with an electric whisk set at a high speed. This will take about 2 minutes.

Now slowly add the syrup, letting it flow down the sides of the bowl, while continuing to beat. Add any required flavouring - vanilla is best - at this stage. Lower the speed of the mixer and continue beating until the icing is fluffy and stands up in peaks like meringue. If it becomes too hard, add a few drops of hot water. Use without delay.

Sufficient to ice the top and sides of 6 x 8-inch/20-cm cakes, or, if tops only are iced, 9 x 8-inch/20-cm cakes

Pineapple or Orange Filling

2 teaspoons/2 x 5 ml spoons grated lemon rind (or orange rind)
1 pint/600 ml pineapple juice (or orange juice)
3 eggs, beaten
5 oz/150 g granulated sugar
3 oz/75 g cornflour
1 pint/600 ml water
2 oz/50 g butter

Allow the lemon (or orange) rind to infuse in the pineapple juice (or orange juice) for 1 hour.

Strain the juice. Beat together in a bowl the eggs, sugar and cornflour, and add the strained fruit juice and water.

Pour into a double boiler and cook, stirring constantly, for about 20 minutes. Beat in the butter, then allow to cool before using.

Colour if liked, but this is not usually necessary.

BISCUITS AND COOKIES

Often people cannot tell the difference between a biscuit and a cookie; a cookie is a softer textured biscuit, whereas a biscuit is thin and crisp. Both biscuits and cookies, when home-made, are extremely popular with customers to eat with their mid-morning cups of coffee. Have a tray or large plate of biscuits, cookies, cakes and scones and let your customers help themselves, so that plates of uneaten food are not left on the tables, to become fingered or contaminated by cigarette smoke and ash.

Refrigerator cookies are a useful base from which to make a variety of delicious biscuits. The cookie paste is rolled into a long 'sausage' and stored in the refrigerator then cut and baked as required (page 177).

Chocolate Crumbles

10 oz/275 g butter or margarine
1 lb/500 g Barbados sugar
10 oz/275 g granulated sugar
2 eggs, beaten
¼ pint/150 ml milk
1 teaspoon/1 x 5 ml spoon vanilla essence
1 lb 10 oz/750 g plain flour
1 teaspoon/1 x 5 ml spoon salt
2 teaspoons/2 x 5 ml spoons baking powder
2 teaspoons/2 x 5 ml spoons bicarbonate of soda
12 oz/350 g couverture chocolate, chopped finely

Cream together the butter and sugars, until light and fluffy. Beat in the eggs.

Add the vanilla essence to the milk.

Sift together the dry ingredients, and add to the creamed mixture alternately with the milk. Stir in the chopped chocolate, and mix thoroughly.

Drop spoonfuls of the mixture, well apart, on greased baking trays.

Bake in a moderately hot oven, mark 6, 400°F/200°C, for 10-15 minutes. Cool slightly before lifting from trays.

Makes about 48

Oatmeal and Raisin Cookies

10 oz/275 g raisins (soaked overnight)
8 oz/225 g butter or margarine
1 lb/500 g soft brown sugar
2 eggs, beaten
1 lb/500 g plain flour
2 teaspoons/2 x 5 ml spoons baking powder
2 teaspoons/2 x 5 ml spoons ground cinnamon
½ teaspoon/½ x 5 ml spoon salt
1 teaspoon/1 x 5 ml spoon bicarbonate of soda
⅓ pint/200 ml milk
12 oz/350 g rolled oats

Remember to soak the raisins overnight; they may be soaked in a little cold tea if there is some left over.

Cream together the butter and soft brown sugar, until light and fluffy.

Beat in the eggs thoroughly.

Sift together the flour, baking powder, cinnamon and salt. Add the bicarbonate of soda to the milk.

Add the flour and milk alternately to the creamed mixture. Stir in the raisins and oats.

Drop spoonfuls of mixture onto greased baking trays, spacing them well apart.

Bake in a moderately hot oven, mark 5, 375°F/190°C, for 15-20 minutes. Leave a little while on the trays before lifting them onto a wire rack to cool.

Makes about 50

Cornflake Macaroons

2 egg whites
½ teaspoon/½ x 5 ml spoon salt
7 oz/200 g caster sugar
2 oz/50 g cornflour
4 oz/100 g mixed nuts, chopped
1½ oz/40 g cornflakes, crushed

Beat the egg whites until they are frothy, then add the salt and sugar and mix well. Stir in the remaining ingredients.

Drop spoonfuls of the mixture, well apart, onto trays on which oiled paper or parchment has been placed.

Bake in a moderate oven, mark 4, 350°F/180°C, for 12-15 minutes. These brown quickly and should be a pale golden colour.
Makes 24 x 2-inch/5-cm macaroons

Note: This is a useful recipe, particularly for Coeliacs who cannot tolerate wheat starch and cannot normally eat biscuits and cakes.

Butterscotch Refrigerator Cookies

1¾ lb/850 g plain flour
1 tablespoon/1 x 15 ml spoon baking powder
1 teaspoon/1 x 5 ml spoon salt
1 lb/500 g butter or margarine
2 lb/1 kg soft brown sugar
3 eggs
2 teaspoons/2 x 5 ml spoons butter flavouring

Sift together the flour, baking powder and salt.

Cream together the butter and soft brown sugar, until light and fluffy.

Beat in the eggs and butter flavouring, then fold in the dry ingredients and mix well. This will form a stiff dough.

Mould the dough into a long 'sausage' shape and wrap in greaseproof paper. Place in the refrigerator until ready to bake the biscuits. It will keep for up to four weeks.

To bake, place the 'sausage on a floured board, and cut into slices. Lay these on greased baking trays, and bake in a moderately hot oven, mark 5, 375°F/190°C, for 10 minutes.
Makes about 100

Note: This mixture also freezes well both in the uncooked state and when baked into biscuits.

Ginger Snaps

9 oz/250 g plain flour
1½ teaspoons/1½ x 5 ml spoons ground ginger
2 teaspoons/2 x 5 ml spoons bicarbonate of soda
1 teaspoon/1 x 5 ml spoon salt
4 oz/100 g margarine
12 oz/350 g black treacle

Sift together the flour, ground ginger, bicarbonate of soda and salt.

Heat the treacle in a saucepan, then add the margarine and allow them to melt together. Add to the dry ingredients.

Mix well, then roll in waxed paper or cling film and leave to rest for one hour.

Roll out the dough thinly on a floured board, and cut into circles of 2-inch/5-cm diameter, using a fluted biscuit cutter or gingerbread man cutter.

Place on greased baking trays. Bake in a moderate oven, mark 4, 350°F/180°C, for 10 minutes.

Makes about 40

BREAD, BUNS AND SCONES

You may, of course, want to make your own bread both for use in the tearoom and for counter sales, or you may prefer to use home-made bread just for counter sales and buy in bread for tearoom use. There may be a good local baker nearby who can supply you with freshly baked bread on a regular basis, so it may well be worthwhile making enquiries.

The delicious aroma of newly baked yeast goods can, of course, be a good advertisement for your business. If you would like to make something on the premises, try making your own buns, since they are less time-consuming to make than bread. Muffins will be popular, and are simple to make, during the winter months.

Scones, I think, should always be made fresh each day, on the premises, and they undoubtedly sell well at morning coffee and teatime - particularly if you are able to serve them with home-made jam. Scones always sell well over the counter.

Malt Bread

8 oz/225 g malt
3 lb/1.5 kg strong white flour
4 pints/2.25 litres water
4 lb/1.75 g wholemeal flour
4 oz/100 g fat, melted
2 oz/50 g fresh yeast
1 oz/25 g salt
1 ascorbic acid tablet, crushed

Mix together the malt, 1 lb/500 g strong white flour and the water, and warm to blood heat. Add the melted fat, yeast and salt and mix well together.

Sieve in the remaining white flour, wholemeal flour and the crushed ascorbic acid tablet. Mix thoroughly together. Allow to stand in a warm place for about 30 minutes, or until risen.

Divide into 14 equal pieces and mould them lightly, then place each in a greased low-sided tin. Cover each tin with a warmed 1-lb/500-g loaf tin and leave to prove in a warm place for about 1 hour. When risen, bake in a moderately hot oven, mark 5, 375°F/190°C, for 35-45 minutes.
Makes 14 small loaves

Currant Loaves

7 lb/3 kg strong white flour
2 oz/50 g fresh yeast
3 pints/1.75 litres warm water
3 oz/75 g dried milk powder
½ oz/15 g malt extract
2 oz/50 g honey
6 oz/175 g caster sugar
½ oz/15 g salt
2 ascorbic acid tablets, crushed
1 lb/500 g vegetable fat, melted
2 lb/1 kg currants
4 oz/100 g cut mixed peel
beaten egg

Sieve the flour into a large bowl. Soften the yeast with a little of the warm water.

Mix together the milk powder, malt, honey, sugar and salt and stir in the remaining water. Pour this onto the flour. Add the yeast and crushed ascorbic acid tablets. Stir well, then fold in the melted vegetable fat. Prove in a warm place for 30 minutes, covered with a damp tea towel.

Fold in the currants and mixed peel, then mix well. Divide into 14 pieces.

Mould and knead lightly, then place in greased 1-lb/500-g loaf tins, and leave to rise in a warm place for a further 30 minutes, or until the loaves have doubled in size. Brush tops with egg.

Bake in a hot oven, mark 7, 425°F/220°C, for about 30 minutes, or until golden on top.

Makes 14 x 1-lb/500-g loaves

Dinner Rolls (Never fail recipe!)

2 oz/50 g fresh yeast
¼ pint/150 ml lukewarm water
4 oz/100 g lard
3 teaspoons/3 x 5 ml spoons caster sugar
1 pint/600 ml boiling water
1 egg, beaten
1 lb 10 oz/750 g strong white flour
2 teaspoons/2 x 5 ml spoons salt

Soften the yeast in the lukewarm water.

Place the lard in a large bowl, add the sugar and boiling water, and stir until creamy. Allow to cool to lukewarm.

Stir in the yeast and beaten egg, then mix well. Add the sieved flour and salt and stir to blend the ingredients.

Cover the dough with a large polythene bag and place the dough in the refrigerator for 2 hours. It should double, or even treble, its bulk. The dough may remain in the refrigerator for up to 12 hours.

Divide the dough into 36 pieces and knead them lightly, then place on greased baking trays. Allow to rise again in a warm place for about 2 hours.

Bake in a hot oven, mark 8, 450°F/230°C, for 15 minutes.

Makes 36 rolls

Speedy Bridge Rolls

12 fl oz/350 ml lukewarm water
6 oz/175 g fat, melted
2 tablespoons/2 x 15 ml spoons caster sugar
1 tablespoon/1 x 15 ml spoon salt
2 oz/50 g fresh yeast
2 eggs, beaten
1 lb 10 oz/750 g strong white flour
oil

Place the water, melted fat, sugar and salt in a bowl.

Soften the yeast with a little lukewarm water and add to the bowl, then beat in the beaten eggs.

Stir in the flour and mix thoroughly. Turn the dough onto a floured surface.

With the backs of the hands, flatten the dough so that it fits into two greased tins measuring 8 x 12 inches/20 x 30 cm. Flatten the dough into the tins, then slash the top into 12 finger shapes, brush the tops of each with a little oil, then allow to rise for about 30 minutes, in a warm place.

Bake in a hot oven, mark 7, 425°F/220°C, for about 30 minutes, or until golden brown and thoroughly cooked.

Pull the rolls apart when ready to serve.

Makes 48

Currant Buns

1 pint/600 ml hot milk
8 oz/225 g lard or white fat
8 oz/225 g caster sugar
1 tablespoon/1 x 15 ml spoon salt
4 oz/100 g fresh yeast
1 pint/600 ml cold water
3 eggs, beaten
3 lb/1.5 kg strong white flour
1 teaspoon/1 x 5 ml spoon mixed spice
1 lb/500 g currants (or mixed dried fruit)
granulated sugar and water

Place the hot milk, lard, sugar and salt in the bowl of a mixer, and mix at slow speed.

Blend the yeast to a thin cream with a little of the warm mixture, then add to the bowl. Stir in the cold water and eggs, then add the sieved flour and mixed spice. Mix well. Add the fruit.

Turn out onto a floured surface and shape into 70 buns. Place the buns on greased baking trays, then place the trays in a warm place for 45 minutes, until the buns have risen. Bake in a hot oven, mark 7, 425°F/220°C, for 20 minutes.

While the buns are baking, blend together equal tablespoons/15 ml spoons water and sugar, and dissolve together in a saucepan.

When baked, brush with glaze. Cool.

Makes 70

Note: This dough may also be made into plaits, currant loaves and teacakes.

Hot Cross Buns

For hot cross buns at Easter time, increase the amount of fruit in the recipe for currant buns to 1½ lb/750 g and, before baking, mark the tops with a cross using the back of a knife.

Muffins

1 pint/600 ml hot milk
4 oz/100 g lard or white fat, melted
1 tablespoon/1 x 15 ml spoon salt
2 tablespoons/2 x 15 ml spoons golden syrup
2 oz/50 g fresh yeast
1½ lb/750 g strong white flour
4 tablespoons/4 x 15 ml spoons semolina

Place the milk, lard, salt and golden syrup in the mixer bowl and mix well. Soften the yeast and add it, together with the sieved flour. Blend well but do not knead.

Turn the dough out onto a floured surface, and roll out to ¼ inch/5 mm thickness, and cut with a 3½-inch/8-cm round biscuit cutter.

Sprinkle baking trays with semolina and lay the muffins well apart on the trays. Sprinkle the tops with the remaining semolina, and allow to rise for 1 hour in a warm place.

Cook on a hot oiled griddle or heavy-based frying pan for about 7 minutes on each side. Serve hot and buttered.
Makes 24

Scones

1½ lb/750 g self-raising flour
1 teaspoon/1 x 5 ml spoon salt
8 oz/225 g margarine
2 pints/1.2 litres milk

Sift together the flour and salt into a large bowl. Rub in the margarine, using the tips of the fingers. Stir in the milk to form a soft, but not sticky, dough.

Turn the dough out onto a floured surface, and lightly knead, then roll out to a thickness of about ¼ inch/5 mm. Using a 1½-inch/4-cm cutter, cut into circles and place them on greased baking trays.

Bake in a hot oven, mark 7, 425°F/220°C, for about 10-12 minutes.
Makes about 56 scones

Note: The tops of the scones may be brushed lightly with milk, prior to baking, if a glazed appearance is required.

A little sugar added to the mixture makes the scones nice and brown.

If you have scones left over from the previous day, make sure that they are only served heated up in a covered container. Never serve them stale.

Wholemeal Scones

If wholemeal scones are required, use 75% wholemeal flour and 25% self-raising flour and 2 teaspoons/2 x 5 ml spoons baking powder, to replace all the self-raising flour given in previous recipe.

Sultana Scones

Add 6 oz/175 g sultanas and 4 oz/100 g caster sugar to the rubbed-in mixture, before adding the milk.

Cheese Scones

Add 6 oz/175 g grated strong cheese and a good pinch mustard powder and a good pinch cayenne pepper to the rubbed-in mixture, before adding the milk. These must be served buttered and piping hot for the best results.

Drop Scones

1 lb/500 g plain flour
1 teaspoon/1 x 5 ml spoon salt
2 teaspoons/2 x 5 ml spoons baking powder
1 teaspoon/1 x 5 ml spoon bicarbonate of soda
2 tablespoons/2 x 15 ml spoons caster sugar
2 eggs
3 pints/1.75 litres milk
1 tablespoon/1 x 15 ml spoon cooking oil

Sift together the flour, salt, baking powder, bicarbonate of soda and sugar. Stir in the eggs and milk and beat to make a smooth batter, then stir in the oil. The batter should be slightly thicker than a pancake batter.

Heat a griddle or heavy-based frying pan, and, using a tablespoon/15 ml spoon, drop spoonfuls of the batter on the griddle. When one side is lightly browned and cooked turn over and cook the other side.

Turn out onto a clean tea towel, and keep the drop scones warm in this until ready to butter them and serve.
Makes 15-20

Note: The griddle should be kept scrupulously clean. There is no need to grease the griddle or the pan; there is sufficient oil in the batter.

INDEX